Antevasin

A Yogic Path to Self-Realization & Personal Freedom

Colette Marie

Also written by Colette Marie

Nonfiction

F**k It! Memoirs of an Unconventional Yogi

The Miracle of Plant Medicine and The Practice of Yoga

The Power of Change—Insights from an Unconventional Yogi

Color Blind—The Hidden Truths of a Biracial Identity

Antevasin

A Yogic Path to Self-Realization & Personal Freedom

Lulu Press, Inc.
3101 Hillsborough St.
Raleigh, North Carolina 27607
www.lulu.com

ISBN: 978-1-6671-1174-2

Cover, Book Design and Content by Colette Marie Mccaine
Photos by Colette Marie Mccaine

Printed in the United States of America

Lulu Press, Inc.
3101 Hillsborough St.
Raleigh, North Carolina 27607
www.lulu.com

Contents

In Loving Memory of my father, Herbert Jerome Wilkerson

Opening Thoughts

Since the start of the pandemic, I have been in a state of self-reflection, on and off. Meaning, one day I would be in deep thought, and other days it would be business as usual with some COVID 19 restrictions in place. Naturally, the amount of time I had to myself at the start of the first shut down was just enough time to think. To think about my life, to think about what I have done with my life, to think about who impacted my life, to think about the relationships I have been involved with, to think about the relationship I am presently in, to think about the trauma of my life, the unfavorable outcomes of my life, to think about the poor decisions I have made over the course of my life, to think about the poor decisions others have made in their lives based on how I may have been treated growing up and as an adult, to think about how I spent my life and to think about how I wish to spend the remainder of my life, if I am not struck with this illness which has claimed over 500,000 lives in our own country alone. Moreover, I have spent a lot of time thinking about my own mortality, about death, the act of death, how I would die, who would be responsible for taking care of me, what my finances would be like to financially support me while I am dying or to manage the after math, such as how I would go, either burial or by cremation and how much all of that would cost.

In other words, I have dedicated a great deal of time thinking about how I have lived my life up until this particular moment through to the start and hopeful end of the pandemic. With this in mind, the amount of clarity which materialized due to this prolonged state of self-reflection, self-analysis, self-inquiry and self-realization, I have come up with a unique theory that has occupied my mental sphere for the past number of weeks and months. This theory is not anything new of course. And perhaps there are various social psychological theories which embody the thoughts I have I am not certain. Of course, there is nothing new under the sun as the book of Ecclesiastes states. That said, I am almost certain there are pre-existing theories hypothesized, measured and written by other psychoanalytic greats of our time. However, because my theory is a new string of thoughts that I now discuss with others to gain insight as to how they think or believe about what I share with them, the curiosity continues to grow like a root structure in my mind, blossoming into a great tree, bursting with a plethora of curvy branches, layered with the most vibrant and colorful of leaves. Moreover, my theory is not a theory that may be readily understood at first, potentially. Yet, there is a strong possibility that you will understand immediately, what it is that I mean.

As you read these pages, you will begin to formulate an opinion. Your opinion may be an opinion of yourself, of the content of this book, of the theory itself and or of me, the writer of this book, which could be viewed as complete nonsense. But I am a fan of keeping an open mind when it comes to "theories". Why? Because a "theory", a "plausible or acceptable general principle or body of principles offered to explain phenomena"[1] is considerably, a work-in-progress. Hence, a theory helps to shed light on phenomena that seems unexplainable. A theory allows room for possibility in thought. Notably, a theory can be researched, studied, debated, discussed, and documented. In sum, a theory makes suggestions as to why things are the way they are or may explain the possible reasons as to how and why things are what they are or seemingly are or may be perceived. All of this and more to be said, my working theory is this: we live in a culture of "poor-decision making". Allow me to repeat that. We

---

[1] *Merriam-Webster Dictionary*

live in a culture of "poor-decision making". This is what I landed on after all of my contemplating.

I surmise, based on my life experiences, on the trajectory of my life from birth to now, that roughly, give or take five or ten percent, that the majority of my suffering has been self-inflicted, self-imposed, and self-perpetuated, due to a perpetual flow of poor-decision making in my life. Of course, that is not to say, that somewhere in this steady stream of poor-decision making, I did not make good decisions, because I have. It would be too unfair of me to create a belief structure around this poor-decision making theory, not at all giving myself credit for making some pretty epic decisions in my lifetime. That would be too negative. However, it is fair of me to suggest to myself that much of my suffering has been due to a number of poor-decisions, one after the other, after the other, after the other. Based upon the timeline of my own life, I can see so vividly, so clearly, so crisply, how each poor-decision gave birth to another poor-decision, and yet another poor-decision. Not with judgement but without judgement, seeing this as phenomena rather than an unfortunate series of events for which I have bestowed upon myself. And allow me to be clear. This is by no means a "poor me" description. On the contrary, this is an observational study using my life as the subject of study to determine if my theory is in fact plausible. Naturally, having this kind of conversation with others certainly garners the kind of attention a curious child has when they learn about molecules and cells in a science class.

The level of discourse that transpires between me and the other is most engaging and enjoyable because there is an intelligent debate in play, one that allows for each party to completely reflect, even if for a few seconds or so on one's own life in order to continue debating one side or another, in favor of or against the "Theory of Poor-Decision Making."

Because, as it turns out, one has a hard time dismissing all of the unfavorable outcomes in one's life due to whatever poor decision was made at that time which created the unsavory trajectory that ultimately culminated into an unfavorable outcome. In fact, I will venture to say that about 99.9% of the human population makes poor decisions at one point or another in life. Conversely, about 99.9% of the human population makes good decisions at one point or another in life. That said, what I am interested in is how does one change the landscape of decision-making from perpetually poor, causing all kinds of suffering, to perpetually good or favorable, creating more harmonious outcomes in one's life. What I want to know for myself most specifically is how do I, Colette Marie, begin creating a track record of good decision making that will yield a higher return of favorable outcomes versus the opposite. Because I have already seen what that looks like. I already know what the unfavorable outcomes are. I already know how much suffering a poor-decision can render. I am well aware of the amount of suffering and pain and anguish that is created as a result of making one poor-decision after the other.

Now it is time to change that trajectory. Because now I know just how all of this began in my life. And this is the experimental timeline that is my life, I am going to share with you all, helping you to see yourself in a new light, not in an effort to inspire fear but to inspire change. Considering that all of us co-exist on this planet, engaging with one another, here and there, it is vital to have a firm understanding about why we choose what we choose, why we make the kinds of decisions we make that place us in a multitude of unfavorable outcomes or circumstances, potentially. Of course, there are a number of things which do happen to us that are most concretely beyond our control. However, how we choose to respond to those events is completely up to us and totally within our realm of absolute control. In other words, we have ownership and agency over our own thoughts, actions, words and deeds when it comes to events and situations which happen outside of our bodily and mental control. To believe that we do not have ownership and agency over our own thoughts, actions, words and deeds, places us in a most precarious position, more often than not. Which only adds to the self-imposed suffering.

What I propose through reading this book is to afford yourself the opportunity to use your life as the subject of study in this science experiment in an effort to connect the dots through observational study in order to determine if whether or not the "Theory of Poor-Decision Making" is plausible. If it is plausible, then steps can be taken in creating a new train of thought, a new way of thinking and way of operating emotionally, behaviorally and psychologically. In other words, when the awareness becomes evident based on your own life script and all of the decisions made in the course of your thirty, forty, fifty or sixty years on this earth, you have an opportunity to begin changing the trajectory going forward. That is the gift of awareness. Although, some would argue, awareness can feel like a curse. Perhaps for some it can. And perhaps in some certain situations it could undoubtably feel that way. However, this is merely a perception based on a singular moment in time which will pass. Ultimately, the decision you make in that moment will, like the butterfly effect, generate a set of outcomes, one giving way to the next. Therefore, I do believe that our culture of poor-decision making has spawned from a number of sources both externally and internally, which have become truths for many of us, thereby creating realities which reflect pain, anger, resentment, depression, anxiety, stress, and fear, which are all elements or constituents of suffering, of which are self-imposed, self-perpetuated, and self-inflicted, more often than not. That must change for the sake of your life and for the sake of humanity.

In conclusion, some of you may be wondering what the title of the book means. The title of the book, *antevasin (n.)*, "is formed from two Sanskrit words; ante meaning end, near the end or edge and vasin is to live or one who lives. Hence, an antevasin is "One who lives on the edge" or literally "one who lives at the end". [2] In other words, "it means, 'one who lives at the border.' In ancient times this was a literal description. It indicated a person who had left the bustling center of worldly life to go live at the edge of the forest where the spiritual masters dwelled. The antevasin was not of the villagers anymore - not a householder with a conventional life. But neither was he yet a transcendent - not one of those sages who live deep in the unexplored woods, fully realized. The antevasin was an in-betweener. He was a border-dweller. He lived in sight of both worlds, but he looked toward the unknown. And he was a scholar."[3] In sum, it is the individual who understands the physical world and the spiritual world, who has one foot in one and the other foot in the other, one who straddles the line between two worlds without losing sight of either. It describes the individual as essentially reaching a place of pure *Self Realization* and *Personal Freedom* as the title and subtitle of this book suggests. And that is what this book will help to inspire.

---

[2] Home Page, *Antevasin Design*: antevasin.co.nz/principles/antevasin
[3] Home Page, *Antevasin Design*: antevasin.co.nz/principles/antevasin

Part One —

The Shadow Self

"Taken in its deepest sense, the shadow is the invisible saurian tail that man still drags behind him. Carefully amputated, it becomes the healing serpent of the mysteries."

– Carl Jung

Chapter 1

Genesis of Decisions

Decision making is like any other kind of art form. It takes time, practice, patience and measured mistakes if we shall refer to "those" decisions as "mistakes". I'd prefer to regard them as that which yields an unfavorable outcome. Like learning how to cook, or paint, draw or knit, there is technique involved, a way of connecting with that which you are interacting with, there is form, methodology, there are the proper tools, there is timing, feeling, approach, the materials used to create whatever it is you wish to create. These are the essential elements to crafting ones art. I believe that similarly, the same considerations which contribute to one's craft can be applied to one's decision making. However, the mind is very layered, and contains a number of lenses, filters, parts of the mind such as the conscious mind, subconscious mind and unconscious mind. Making decisions seems relatively easy. And for the most part "making a decision" *is*. On the other hand, making a decision can be difficult depending on what it is one has to decide upon. Yet, more often than not, many of us make decisions as we go a long, without any real thought to the outcome. In sum, our decisions are, more often than not, on the fly, on the spot, in the moment, or made out of fear, anger, stress, pressure, rashness, haste or anxiety. Conversely, some of our decision making may be made out of sound judgement, clear and rational thinking, forethought, forward thinking, creative divergent thinking, clarity of mind, perhaps even pleasure, happiness and or joy. There are all sorts of contributing factors which influence our decisions every moment of every day. But how many of those decisions are conscious decisions and how many of them are not.

For example, according to 2019 Smash Magazine article, "How People Make Decisions", Dr. Susan Weinschenk, Behavioral Scientist, asserts that "research shows that most of our decisions — big or small — are made unconsciously and involve emotion." What's more, Weinschenk states that "by looking at brain activity while making a decision, researchers could predict what choice people would make 7-10 seconds before they themselves were even aware of having made a decision. This means that even when people think they are making a conscious, logical, decision, chances are that they aren't aware that they've already made a decision and that it was unconscious. We aren't even aware of our own process." Weinschenk continues by suggesting that "most of our mental processing is unconscious, and most of our decision-making is unconscious, but that doesn't mean it's faulty, irrational, or bad. We are faced with an overwhelming amount of data (11,000,000 pieces of data come into the brain every second according to Dr. Timothy Wilson in his book "Strangers To Ourselves: Discovering The Adaptive Unconscious") and our conscious minds can't process all of that. In sum, Weinschenk purports that "our unconscious has evolved to process most of the data and to make decisions for us according to guidelines and rules of thumb that are in our best interest most of the time. This is the genesis of "trusting your gut", and most of the time it works!"

The key phrase to take away, in regard to the proposal of good decision making in the context of this book is the phrase "to make decisions… that are in our best interest." But I ask, when we are young, how often does that occur? Most importantly, how often, do we as adults, typically, generally speaking, by and large make decisions with our best interests in mind and at heart? Perhaps you can answer that and say in your mind, that you make good decisions most of the time. And if that is the case, I wish to be like you when I grow up. If not, you are like me wondering where in the timeline of your life did you start making poor decisions and why? Again, this is not a judgement. This is part of the observation process. In essence, what Dr. Weinschenk is sharing with us through this article, is that most of the decisions we make are in fact unconscious decisions well before they become conscious and that most of the time, potentially, we have used our "gut" to guide us to making a decision. That is to say, when we trust our gut, more often than not, we are leading ourselves in the right direction. However, I am questioning the frequency of how often that actually happens in a person's life, on a day-to-day basis. Naturally, I am not suggesting that people don't inherently make good decisions regularly, because that would not be entirely accurate. On the contrary, many people make good gut "feeling" decisions with their best interests in mind. Conversely, there are a number of people who perpetually, for one reason or another, make more poor decisions, than favorable decisions, in their lives on a day-to-day basis. And there is a reason or set of reasons for that trajectory that I wish to explore with you.

When it comes to our day-to-day activities, our engagements, interactions, conversations, events, situations, circumstances, and so forth, decisions are made in either reaction to something or in response to something and the distinction here must be made. For example, some would argue that to "react" is the same to "respond". And according to a variety of dictionary sources, these two words are used interchangeably. However, according to the teachings of mindfulness that is an offshoot of Buddhism, "reaction" and "response" are slightly varied. For instance, to "re" "act" implies the repetitiveness of an action. Simply put, the prefix of "re" means "back" or "again". Therefore, to "react" means to rehearse the same repeat action to an external situation. Whereas, the term response, implies that there is no rehearsal, no repetitive-ness in action, or how one chooses to engage in a situation such as, being fully present, thereby "responding" in the "present moment" of the external stimuli without all of the trauma, emotional luggage, skewed mental lenses, warped perspectives, misconceptions and distortions one might bring to the table. But this is all just, potentially, a lot of pseudo-science talk that some may argue is irrelevant. Perhaps they are correct in their argument. However, it is worth considering, the fact that, when we do "react" to something, that we are virtually "re-enacting" to something, with a repetitiveness associated with it. That we are replaying the same old set of emotions and feelings over and over without thought, without question, without ever wondering where all our emotions are coming from.

In fact, I am of the opinion that much of the emotional outpour in a single moment of a situation are more often than not, displaced. Meaning, one may be over-reacting, which happens all of the time. And happen without question. Which suggests that the individual has yet to become aware of one's own emotional frequency and energy output when faced with an uncomfortable circumstance before making a decision on the spot, which could, potentially render an unfavorable outcome because a decision was a "reaction" to something, or made out of haste, and not clear and calm thinking. As a result, based on my own life experience, another set of circumstances are born from one hasty decision after another hasty decision, and so on. Hence, the stream of poor-decision making without thought, are based on imbalanced emotions and skewed perspectives, old wounds, unresolved traumas, old pain, and suffering, all crashing into each other like multicar pile up on the highway. This psychological crash scenario has been very much part of our societal landscape of interacting with one another, to events and most importantly with interacting with our own psyche. I have finally reached a point in my life where I am examining the genesis of my decision making, because I see now, the error of my ways. Of course, that is not to say, that at some point in life between now and the day I die, I will not make a sound decision. I am certain I will make one here and there from emotional triggers in the moment of a discussion or of an event. However, the ratio at which I intend to make poor decisions at this point in life will be significantly lower than they were over the past forty-eight years of my life.

I think of it like this. If I want to invest my money so that I can plan for retirement, yielding a healthy return on my investments, I would, consult with an Investment Advisor with a consistent track record of making good investment decisions to ensure that I am making sound investment choices in an effort to see a healthy return on my investments. This kind of thinking is regarded as smart financial planning. A kind of thinking that is highly praised in our culture, because in truth, cash is king. Conversely, I would not consult with an Investment Advisor who has a track record of making poor investment decisions, that may cause people to go into debt, or lose money, or owe the IRS, finding financial shortcuts in hopes to gain a quick buck, which never ends well. Based on this scenario, one could apply the same logic to decision making in a sense. Of course, Dr. Weinschenk asserts that "there are hundreds of decisions we make every day, and we don't do a logical think through of everyone." Using the investment advisor as the analogy in this context, I find it worthwhile to apply similar reasoning even though, Dr. Weinschenk, in her thirty years as a behavior scientist, believes using critical thinking or creative divergent thinking or logic as it is discussed here, are rarely used in the decision-making process. And she is absolutely correct. I, however, believe we can all adopt new way of approaching the decision-making faculties, so that you or I, for example, can begin changing the direction of our lives for the better, as a result, of a series of good decisions. Because, I prefer to have my outcomes be consistently favorable if I can help it. I would like my investment into good decision-making yield more favorable outcomes on a consistent basis. Because I know in my heart, mind and "gut" that this way of thinking certainly alters the course one is on, going forward.

Furthermore, I know based on my own life experience, using it as the subject of analysis in this book, that it is possible to train the mind to think a particular way. Again, that is not to say things do not happen in life because we all know that they do. We cannot control that which is outside of our own body and mind. But we most certainly can control our thoughts, our actions, how we chose to interact with something or someone, our words and our intentions. Therefore, it is possible to actually do the thing which Dr. Weinschenk believes typically cannot be done or is not done. I like to think of it this way. Everything in life, from the way I see it, exists in percentages from zero percent to one hundred percent. Everything we do, including how we live our lives spans the line between zero and one hundred. For example, I eat plant-based food about 50% of the time and eat animal protein the other 50% of the time. This would be my 50/50 diet. It once used to be 80% plant-based and 20% animal protein. I was consistent with the 80/20 diet plan. Another example would be I exercise about five days a week out of seven. That means I exercise about 70% of the time, while I rest or relax for about 30% of the time. It just so happens that the 70/30 ratio works for me. I used to work out 7 days a week in the past which is 100% of the time which was not sustainable for a long-term plan. Then when the pandemic hit, I went from 70% of the time working out at the gym to 0% of the time at the gym. Then I continued eating about 2,500 to 3,000 calories per day for several months. Ultimately, I began to gain weight. As much as twenty additional pounds over my typical weight range.

With the percentages scenario in mind that is used for a number of things in everyday mathematics and computations, we can surmise that our very lives do in fact exist in percentages. This is how we weight the pros and cons of a variety of things and take into consideration the unknown variables which may alter the course we are and perhaps derail us or conversely, create a new opportunity for something. It really, all depends on you or me, and how we "respond" to this or that in the moment. All of this to be said, and keeping the story of percentages in mind, I believe decision-making can be considered in this manner. For instance, my decision-making over the years was 80% poor and 20% favorable. In some cases, during my youth, my decision making estimated at about 90% poor and 10% favorable. Now, my decision-making ratio has flipped to my favor. Meaning, my decision-making ratio, is at present, about 90% good decisions to 10% poor at this stage in my life. I can confidently say that my decisions now are consistently good decisions rendering really favorable outcomes. But this is a whole new way of living, thinking and being. I had to really work hard just to get to this point and there is still more work to be done. The learning never ends.

Chapter 2

Psychosocial Constructs

In this chapter we are going to unpack what psychosocial constructs are in our lives, based upon the psychosocial theory and how this theory has become a construct in many ways, in and of itself. But first we have to understand what "psychosocial theory" means at some level to have a foundation to work with going forward. That said, psychosocial theory "explains changes in self-understanding, social relationships, and one's relationship to society from infancy through later life."[4] Furthermore, there are six basic concepts in psychosocial theory. For example, "(a) stages of development, (b) psychosocial crises, (c) the central process for resolving the psychosocial crisis, (d) the radius of significant relationships, (e) prime adaptive ego qualities, and (f) core pathologies."[5] Now all of this sounds like a lot. And there is much to comb through with each of these concepts. However, we are only going to touch on the basic fundamental aspects of each as they pertain to the decision-making process all in an effort to gain more clarity of oneself and of owns path in life. Again, breaking all of this down is to help us get from here to there, from unawareness to self-realization and personal freedom. But we have to understand how the mind works at its core, to better navigate the terrain of our own consciousness and psyche.

In a nutshell, "psychosocial theories explore the psychosocial crisis of adolescence, personal identity vs identity confusion. This concept highlights the need for individuals to find self-definition as well as a sense

---

[4] Science Direct: sciencedirect.com/topics/psychology/psychosocial-theory
[5] Science Direct: sciencedirect.com/topics/psychology/psychosocial-theory

of meaning and purpose that will guide decisions as they transition into adulthood."[6] The key word in this phrase is "decisions". In truth, at the core of our experiences, to perhaps find "meaning" and "purpose", to understand our "personal identity" whatever that is, or to "find self-definition," decisions must be made, choices must be made. Simply put, one cannot get from here to there without making a decision. One cannot figure out what comes next or which direction to go, or which path to take or which class to take in college without making a decision based upon all of the layers of one's mind and personhood. Moreover, these layers of mind and of personhood come from more decisions which were made when one was a child, as well as by those who took care of you when you were young, who cared for you and who influenced your mind. In fact, our first interactions with people in the world and how we make decisions come from those closest to us, such as our parents or guardians, grandparents, siblings, friends, teachers, doctors, pastors, ministers, members of the church or other religious meeting places, our community and neighborhood in which we live. These are the first external encounters we have access to the moment we pop into this world.

These are the people who we formulate bonds with and who influence our thinking from a very early age. And depending on their decision-making processes, who knows what kind of decisions these adults were making when we were too young to understand anything. I am not saying they were poor decisions, but one has to ask or at the very least question how often these adults made good decisions. I am going to share a truth that you may not agree with, but it is my theory I am hashing out here with you in hopes that by using my life as the example, you may gain

---

[6] Psychosocial Theory, *Science Direct*:
sciencedirect.com/topics/psychology/psychosocial-theory

insight into the theory for your consideration. Therefore, based on the culture of "poor-decision making theory", knowing at this point what this theory implies, it is clear, that I am the result of poor decision making. Here's why. Firstly, my mother decided to move out of the house, live on her own, get a job and take care of herself. That was all good, but stemmed from poor environmental circumstances, circumstances which were highly unfavorable and abusive in nature. Her action to leave was in reaction to the events which unfolded daily in her home. Similarly, my father was in and out of relationships, moving here and there, making a series of poor decisions in his own life, which all led to the intersection of my mother and father. Both of whom should not have married as their marriage was extremely tumultuous and unkind to put it mildly. Both of whom should not have gone as far as having a child. Meaning, for whatever reason, my mother chose to take fertility drugs in order to get pregnant.

The medical intervention coupled with their unbalanced marriage and unharmonious household made the experience of bringing a life into this world that much more stressful. Add to that physical abuse, unresolved traumas from both parents, anger, resentment and pain from both parents, the biological cocktail which was brewing in my mother's belly was the result of one poor decision after the other. Nine months later, I arrive to the world of mounting hostilities and unresolved traumas. Interestingly enough, the infertility drugs created a birth defect which was a cleft-palate and loss of blood for which I needed a transfusion. My beginnings on this earth were sketchy at best. It was certainly touch and go for a little while. But as it happens to be, I was meant for this world and so my little infant self, pulled through. Well at least for a short while. As you can see, the events which precipitated my mother and father's intersection, then gradual coupling, then marriage, then family, were all effects of decisions. In their cases, given their background and their lives up until that moment in time that they meet and manage to marry and have a child, their decisions were a mix of good and not so good. Their marriage for certain was a poor decision given the negative activity which transpired between then most days and nights of their marriage. There were some good decisions sprinkled in there. I do know that in the beginning, "I" was not born of "good-decision" making. Add to that, a birth defect, and other possible mental illnesses including, ADHD.

The point here, is that given my theory and knowing about their past and the struggle of my infancy, I use my life as the example of a series of decisions culminating into a life. And the psychosocial constructs for which I speak are just that. Constructs. Constructs in which almost every human being subscribes to, based on our entry into this life and those around us and their systems of beliefs, their decisions, their feelings, thoughts, actions, words, their unresolved trauma, their pain, their suffering, their accomplishments, happiness, their triumphs, their love and so on. To better clarify, "in philosophy, a construct is an object which is ideal, that is, an object of the mind or of thought, meaning that its existence may be said to depend upon a subject's mind."[7] It may seem as though I am only focusing on the negative of one's life or choices in life or decisions. On the contrary, I am focused on the fact that many people across the globe suffer as a result of a steady stream of poor decisions made in life, all of which began at infancy, through childhood, young adulthood or adolescence and into adulthood. Hence, as we recently learned that "psychosocial theories explore the psychosocial crisis of adolescence, personal identity vs identity confusion. This concept highlights the need for

---

[7] *Wikipedia*

individuals to find self-definition as well as a sense of meaning and purpose that will guide decisions as they transition into adulthood."[8]

All I am suggesting with this theory I have swirling around in my head is that perhaps, just perhaps, many of us have been going about this all wrong from the start. Clearly, not every single human being has a track record of making poor decisions. And even in the series of poor decisions a number of us have made, we have also made a number of good and favorable decisions resulting in favorable or meaningful outcomes in life. But what if, from the beginning, a different trend can be set with making good decisions rather than poor? What if, we as human beings some-how learn the art of good decision making. After all, it is a skill, much like interpersonal communication is a skill, critical thinking is a skill, carpentry is a skill, information technology is a skill, solving equations is a skill, financial literacy is also a skill. Speaking of which, now and days, more and more adults are teaching their children how to be financially literate people, teaching them what it means to save, how to budget, to open up bank accounts, a line of credit and how to manage their credit so that their credit scores improve over time, which ultimately places these young people in a very financially sound place from the start. That means, that these young people will have excellent credit by the time they are in their late teens or early twenties. Essentially, their borrowing power increases Their ability to buy a home is prevalent, and their ability to finance a car is attainable.

If adults can spend the time to help their child learn the art of finances early in life, which by the way is a very good decision on the part of the parents, what's to stop parents and or guardians from teaching their children how to make good decisions in life through scenario exercises,

---

[8] Psychosocial Theory, *Science Direct*:
sciencedirect.com/topics/psychology/psychosocial-theory

generally speaking? What's more, if schools have a curriculum which helps the child learn about history, science, language arts, sociology, foreign language, literature, and more, why not add, "good decision making" as a course in the public and or private school systems across the country? If this kind of thing is unattainable within the home, why not have it be part of the child's "whole" education? I believe that Financial Literacy should also be part of the child's "whole" education as well. Both of these aspects for which I speak should be part of the child's entire educational career starting in Pre-K. Because the two things which young people struggle with from the very beginning in life are finances and making good decisions. If these two items are not part of the child's overall everyday landscape of life, the lessons which need to be learned will potentially not be learned until later down the line if ever, if someone does not come along to educate those individuals. Or perhaps until that person experiences a number of unfavorable events in life reaching a point of changing one's life around for the better. Because that does happen from time to time.

When I sit and think about the "what if's" in my life, from early years, I wonder which direction my life would have taken as a result. Of course, my life is where it is now. I am happy with my life as it is right now because I did a lot of inner work to arrive to a place where I am making consistently good decisions be them financial, educational, physical, mental, emotional, etcetera. I am making a concerted effort to ensure a more favorable outcome by consciously thinking about my next step, weighing the pros and cons. From where I stand, there is nothing wrong with operating in this fashion on a regular basis. Heck. This is why we have the industry of Risk Management. For example, "risk management is the process of identifying, assessing and controlling threats to an organization's capital and earnings. These threats, or risks, could stem from a wide variety of sources, including financial uncertainty, legal liabilities, strategic management errors, accidents and natural disasters."[9] What's more, "by implementing a risk management plan and considering the various potential risks or events before they occur, an organization can save money and protect their future. This is because a robust risk management plan will help a company establish procedures to avoid potential threats, minimize their impact should they occur and cope with the results. This ability to understand and control risk enables organizations to be more confident in their business decisions. Furthermore, strong corporate governance principles that focus specifically on risk management can help a company reach their goals."[10]

Let us review some of the language used in the previous paragraphs: (1) "by implementing a risk management plan and consider the various potential risks or events before they occur, a" person "can save money", time, avoid unnecessary stresses, "and protect their future." (2) "This is because a robust risk management plan will help" a person "establish procedures to avoid potential threats, minimize their impact should they occur and cope with the results." (3) "This ability to understand and control risk enables" a person "to be more confident in their business" personal and professional "decisions." All I did here was change the words from "company" and "organization" to "a person", to add the personal aspect to the language and the description. When I read this the way I have it written, it all totally makes sense to me and gives me pause to think about how to consider approaching the decision-making process. I am not saying I will automatically start thinking along these lines without fail. Of course, time is required to gain practice at doing so. People are not essentially born making good financial decisions or assessing their risk. These things are

---

[9] *TechTarget*: searchcompliance.techtarget.com/definition/risk-management
[10] *TechTarget*: searchcompliance.techtarget.com/definition/risk-management

taught, learned, potentially through life experience or through some kind of formal learning institution, course, certification or education platform. Therefore, I do believe that in the end, it is very, very, possible to teach young people how to make good decisions therefore setting them up for a more successful future, potentially. At least, that is how I see it, given my life now and where it was forty or so years ago. Hence, the psychosocial construct could include "good decision-making" as a course program in built within the sphere and scope of learning through the developmental years of a child.

Chapter 3

The Human Psyche

In the *opening thoughts* of this book, I mentioned the "Shadow Self", an aspect of the "Shadow Archetype", a concept that Swiss Psychiatrist Carl Jung introduces in his scientific research and study of the human psyche. For example, according to Jung, "The *shadow* archetype is composed primarily of the elements of ourselves that we consider to be negative. We do not show this side of the self to the outside world as it can be a source of anxiety or shame. The shadow may contain repressed ideas or thoughts which we do not wish to integrate into our outward *persona*, but these must be resolved in order to achieve *individuation*. However, it may also include positive traits, such as perceived weaknesses (for example, empathy) which may not fit into the 'toughness' that a person wants to present as a part of their persona."[11] The "Shadow Self" like Carl Jung's "Shadow Archetype", pertains to a side of one's consciousness, one that is hidden away from others, one that contains all of the unresolved trauma's, pain, fear, self-doubt and so on. This is the "dark side" of the individual, much like Darth Vader, who was instrumental in the advancement of the Dark Side of the Force.

This aspect of our consciousness is claimed to be part of the collective unconscious part of the mind. For instance, according to Jung, "the personal unconscious contains memories which we are unaware we still possess, often as a result of repression. As we exist in a conscious state, we do not have direct access to our personal unconscious, but it emerges

---

[11] Carl Jung: *Archetypes and Analytical Psychology.*
psychologistworld.com/cognitive/carl-jung-analytical-psychology

in our dreams or in a hypnotic state of regression."[12] What's more, "Jung proposed that we are each born with a collective unconscious. This contains a set of shared memories and ideas, which we can all identify with, regardless of the culture that we were born into or the time period in which we live. We cannot communicate *through* the collective unconscious, but we recognize some of the same ideas innately, including archetypes."[13] This is where the concept of the "Shadow Self"/ "Shadow Archetype" comes from. And does any of this matter? It matters because it provides context into the human psyche with regards to how we behave, how we interact with others, how we think, how we feel, how we respond or react to things, how we communicate with others, what we think about ourselves, how we cope with life's problems and issues as they arise, how we cope with loss, how we manage our own behaviors, feelings and emotions, all of which come from various parts of the mind. In other words, the inner landscape of our mind is not localized. The inner landscape of our mind spans across three parts of the psyche: the ego, the personal unconscious and the collective unconscious. However, there is a fourth part. That is the "subconscious" part of the brain.

For example, according to Dr. Joseph Murphy, he believes that "you have only one mind, but that one mind possesses two distinct and characteristic functional parts. The frontier that separates the two is well known to students of the mind. The two functions of your mind are essentially different from each other. Each has its own separate and distinct attributes and powers. Many names have been used to distinguish the two functions of the mind. These include the objective and the subjective mind, the conscious and the subconscious mind, the waking and the sleeping

---

[12] Carl Jung: *Archetypes and Analytical Psychology.*
psychologistworld.com/cognitive/carl-jung-analytical-psychology
[13] Carl Jung: *Archetypes and Analytical Psychology*

mind, the surface and the deep self, the voluntary and the involuntary mind, the male and the female mind, and many others."[14] What's more, Dr. Murphy subscribes to the belief of the *Law of Cause and Effect*, which also applies to how one thinks or what one's thoughts are on a day-to-day basis. What he suggests based on the *Law of Cause and Effect* is that whatever a person is habitually thinking, those thoughts become part of one's external landscape that is one's reality. In other words, what Dr. Murphy is alleging is that "every thought is a cause, and every condition is an effect." Moreover, "this is the reason it is so essential that you take charge of your thoughts. In that way, you can bring forth only desirable conditions."[15]

Circling back, according to Carl Jung, "the human psyche is the whole mind, including the conscious and the unconscious. Jung's theory states that each person's psyche is comprised of three components:

1. *Ego*

The hub of consciousness that forms all unrepressed perceptions, thoughts, feelings and memories. When Donna walks into a room, her ego perceives the color of the walls, the people in the room and what they're doing and the song playing in the background. But the ego can only hold a select amount of information and the remaining data sinks into the unconscious.

2. *Personal unconscious*

The experiences and memories unique to the individual that are not currently in, but are readily available to, the conscious mind. For example, maybe Donna feels uncomfortable in the room where she just walked. She doesn't like it, but she's not sure why. It just gives her a bad feeling. Perhaps

---

[14] *The Power of Your Subconscious Mind*, Dr. Joseph Murphy, *The Duality of Mind* (p. 6)

[15] *The Power of Your Subconscious Mind*, Dr. Joseph Murphy, *The Conscious and Subconscious Minds* (p.7)

it's because the walls are the same color as the hospital room where her grandmother died. She doesn't consciously associate the room with her grandmother dying, but she has bad feelings because her personal unconscious is at work.

3. *Collective unconscious*

The universal experiences and memories shared by all humans - the blueprints for life that allow us to adapt and survive. The collective unconscious is further comprised of archetypes, or modes of thought that belong to all of humanity. The hero and villain, son and father, strong and weak - these are all archetypes. Donna also feels uneasy in the room because the decorations are almost all black. She associates black with evil and white with good, like many people do. This is an example of archetypes."[16]

Regarding the *Law of Cause and Effect*, that simply means that for every action there is an equal reaction. Similarly, *Causality*, "(also referred to as causation, or cause and effect) is influence by which one event, process, state or object (a *cause*) contributes to the production of another event, process, state or object (an *effect*) where the cause is partly responsible for the effect, and the effect is partly dependent on the cause. In general, a process has many causes, which are also said to be *causal factors* for it, and all lie in its past. An effect can in turn be a cause of, or causal factor for, many other effects, which all lie in its future."[17] Therefore, it stands to reason that with every kind of "decision" made poor or good, there is an equal reaction to one's decision. Another way to look at it is, that with every choice, there is a consequence of that choice. Of course, the term consequence has gotten a "bad-wrap" because of its negative association,

---

[16] Carl Jung's Theories: Personality, Psyche & Dreams:
study.com/academy/lesson/carl-jungs-theories-lesson-quiz.html
[17] *Wikipedia*: en.wikipedia.org/wiki/Causality

like when we were children and we were scolded by our parents if we did something bad, we were told that there are "consequences to your actions." I know that I hated hearing that. But they were correct. There are consequences to our actions, be them good or not so good. Similarly, with every action there is a thought which generated the action in the first place. An action begins with a single thought to act on ones thought. In sum, a decision is made in a moment. And who knows what kind of time went into that decision. That said, knowing more about the law of cause and effect and knowing more about the functions of the psyche to some extent, one could argue that our decisions do in fact impact our day-to-day, that they do produce an effect, that they do create a reaction, that there will be a consequence to that decision, and that depending on what is contained within our conscious mind, subconscious mind, or unconscious mind and even our collective unconscious mind as Jung suggests we have, regarding our Shadow Self, a single decision if it is poor in nature will undoubtably generate a poor outcome.

Therefore, if we do not have the proper skills of making good decisions instilled early in life, coupled with our external factors, we may in fact set up a trajectory of perpetual, perhaps long-term poor decision making for which one's life course will be negatively impacted, quite possibly. Of course, this is all just a working theory. I am not suggesting that what I propose is "fact". However, using my life as the observational study tool, I can see how this theory is relevant. Reviewing the lives of my family members and friends and strangers I meet in the street I can see how this theory is relevant. I am not saying we are all bad people. Of course, we are not. What I am saying is that we lacked the skills to exercise good decision making, and our external factors may have been negative, stressful, which added to the potential of making poor decisions from an early age and that we lacked the support and or tutelage to learn another path as we transitioned into adulthood. And I will repeat the phrase regarding what Jung suggests. "Psychosocial theories explore the psychosocial crisis of adolescence, personal identity vs identity confusion. This concept highlights the need for individuals to find self-definition as well as a sense of meaning and purpose that will guide decisions as they transition into adulthood."[18]

Taking into account all of what has been offered here in this particular chapter, you and I can surmise that the hidden parts, the more negative parts, the shadow parts, of our consciousness, the unresolved trauma, the repressed memories, the triggers, the subconscious thought patterns, the conscious thought patterns, all of it, all contribute to how we make decisions and choices in life on a day-to-day, minute-to-minute basis. And knowing now, based on what you have read thus far, you can estimate that given the information presented, you can begin to shift how you choose to operate going forward with regards the quality of your decisions. I, too, have more insight about the quality of decisions I make in my life, even down to the smallest kind of decision, such as what kind of shoes to wear before I go out for a hike, or a walk with the dog, or whether or not to bring an umbrella with me if there is rain in the forecast. These are miniscule examples to illustrate the decision-making process and the quality of each decision which may render a better outcome.

Yet, there is more to consider when it comes to the timeline of our own lives. For example, previously, I mentioned "life course" theory as it pertains to poor decision-making and the consequences of perpetual poor decision-making. According to Criminology Professor, Dr. Larry J. Siegel, he purports that "according to the life course view, even as toddlers, people

---

18 Psychosocial Theory, *Science Direct*:
sciencedirect.com/topics/psychology/psychosocial-theory

begin relationships and behaviors that will determine their entire life course. As children they must learn to conform to social rules and function effectively in society. Later as teens, they are expected to being thinking about careers, complete their schools, leave their parent's home, enter the workforce. In young adulthood, people find permanent relationships, eventually marry, and begin their own families. These transitions are expected to take place in an orderly fashion."[19] Dr. Seigel continues to share a view of how criminality may manifest as a result of the major transitions being disrupted. Moreover Dr. Seigel asserts that "those who are already at risk because of socioeconomic problems or family dysfunction are the most susceptible during these awkward transitions. The cumulative impact of these disruptions sustains criminality from childhood into adulthood."[20] Though what Dr. Seigel is discussing is centered around criminology, the theory remains applicable in the sense that, a child's life course is determined upon the decisions which are made and the external factors and or circumstances which influence a child's choices, as they transition into adolescence and adulthood, as Carl Jung has also purported with a number of his theories.

Perhaps you now may be asking yourself what is the significance of what Dr. Seigel suggests regarding criminality and the "life course theory"? The significance to Seigel's "life course theory" is that anyone's life course requires "decision-making". A person's life course and trajectory of their life requires choices to be made and therefore actions to be taken as a result of one's choice and decision. A life course cannot be a life course without choosing a life course to begin with. Therefore, for a life course to be a successful life course or render a more favorable life course, better

---

[19] Seigel, Larry J., "Life Course Theory": *Criminology the Core*, (p. 289)
[20] Seigel, Larry J., "Life Course Theory": *Criminology the Core*, (p. 289)

decision-making is of the upmost importance in a young person's life. And if this skill is not promoted or at the very least introduced within the home from a very early age, as well as reinforced through leading by example, then the child will, more-often-than-not, potentially, be unable, to make a clear distinction between a poor decision or a favorable decision. Hence, the consequences of one's choices may either be negative or positive depending on the choice made.

Chapter 4

Philosophy of Mind

Thus far, we have examined some of the sociological, psychological and criminological aspects of the human psyche, of psychosocial constructs, and of the genesis of decision-making. Now we are going to explore the philosophical aspects of the mind as it pertains to the decision-making process. Because all of these branches of study tie into the variety of points I wish to make in support of my theory. For example, as I mentioned before, Carl Jung believed that the human psyche had three parts: the ego, the personal unconscious and the collective unconscious. According to the Yoga Sutra's of Patanjali, Sri Swami Satchidananda states that "there are three different levels of the mind: Ahamkara or Ego, the "I" feeling, Buddhi; the discriminative faculty or intellect and Manas: the desiring part of the mind, which gets attracted to outside things through the senses."[21]

According to Carl Jung, "the personal unconscious contains memories which are unaware we still possess, often as a result of repression."[22] According to the Sutras the "entire outside world is based on your thoughts and mental attitude." Therefore, "the entire world is your own projection."[23] In contrast, "Jung noted that we each have a *persona* - an identity which we wish to project to others. He used the Latin term, which can refer either to a person's personality the mask of an actor, intentionally,

---

[21] The Yoga Sutras of Patanjali: *Portion on Contemplation*: (p. 4)
[22] Carl Jung: Archetypes and Analytical Psychology:
psychologistworld.com/cognitive/carl-jung-analytical-psychology
[23] The Yoga Sutras of Patanjali: *Portion on Contemplation*: (p. 5)

as the persona can be constructed from archetypes in the collective unconscious or be influenced by ideas of social roles in society." [24] Comparatively, according to the Sutras and with regard to Ahamkara or Ego or "I" feeling, Patanjali focuses on what may cause one to feel bound in the context of the "I" feeling. For example, Swami Satchidananda states that "as the mind; so, the man, bondage or liberation are in your own mind."[25] In other words, he says "if you feel bound, you are bound. If you feel liberated, you are. Things outside neither bound nor liberate you; only your attitude towards them does that."[26]

These comparative views are substantially aligned when we think about how one perceives both their inner world, their thoughts and decisions and the outside world, their reality and experiences, of which are an effect of a person's decision -making. In essence, what the Sutras are basically saying is that your thoughts dictate your reality, your attitude towards this or that dictates the quality of your experiences. Hence, your decision will have a direct impact on the quality of the outcome in which you experience in any given situation. Therefore, the quality of your decision or of my decision is vital when we realize how impactful an outcome may be both in the short-term and long-term. Because simply put, each decision has both a short-term effect and long-term effect. For example, I chose to take up smoking in my life which started in my twenties. It started off as a casual thing, sporadically engaging in social activities which included cigarettes which later became a full-blown addiction problem as years passed. Only to begin experiencing dry cough, accumulated mucous in my lungs, tender throat, acne and hormone

---

[24] Carl Jung: Archetypes and Analytical Psychology:
psychologistworld.com/cognitive/carl-jung-analytical-psychology
[25] The Yoga Sutras of Patanjali: *Portion on Contemplation*: (p. 5)
[26] The Yoga Sutras of Patanjali: *Portion on Contemplation*: (p. 5)

imbalance, to the point of experiencing infertility. In sum, a choice I made at twenty-two, became problematic for me in my thirties when I was diagnosed with "unexplained infertility". Meaning, no one really knew why but the smoking certainly did not help increase fertility. A decision which spawned a long-term effect.

This is one example using my life as the test subject to illustrate how far reaching a decision can be. Moreover, some people I know began smoking when they were teenagers and later was diagnosed with Chronic Obstructive Pulmonary Disease. A disease which materialized in their forties, from a decision which was made in their teens. Again, just another example of how far reaching a decision can be. In some, more extreme cases, people I know had been diagnosed with Lung Cancer and passed away. Conversely, a young person decides that they want to go to Berkeley University, then go to Law School and later become a Judge. And so, they begin cultivating good study habits, attend study groups, get involved in school activities, begin taking honors classes and Advanced Placement classes and start working on their Standardized tests to prepare for college applications. Decision, after decision, after decision, she gets accepted at Berkeley University, goes to law school and later becomes a Judge. This scenario is positive example of a series of good decisions which yielded a set of positive long-term effects. One might ask, well why did she decide all of those things and why did I and others who chose to smoke, choose to smoke? I would have to respond by saying, good damn question. Why did we decided those things and why did she decide what she decided?

Perhaps, it is possible, knowing her family, and her family background, she was taught early in life about choosing things that will improve the quality of her life, which happen to include getting an education, as education was very much pushed and pursued in her household by both parents. In fact, both siblings were successful in that area and both have gone on to do great things in their lives. That is not to say, that somewhere in the timeline of their lives they did not make poor decisions. I am certain that they did one time or another for one reason or another. However, the track record of their good decision making outweighs the poor choices made in their lives, potentially. In fact, one could argue, and we do not know all of the details and facts, but one could argue, based on my percentage's theory, that this individual who became a judge might have made good decisions about 80% of the time, perhaps 90% of the time, leaving room for error and being a human being, to making poor decisions 10% - 20% of the time. It is plausible. I cannot, with absolute certainty say, that is the case for her. However, it does prove that creating a consistent path of good decisions does in fact create a more harmonious and successful set of outcomes, potentially. And I keep using that word, "potentially" because, it is a potential. It is not an absolute certainty but a probable potentiality.

Using my own life as the subject of study, choosing the yogic path in 2005 was the one of the best decisions I have made in the timeline of my life. A decision which was made over fifteen years ago continues to render positive outcomes in life. It is the gift that keeps on giving. That is not to say, that somewhere during the past fifteen or so years, I did not make poor decisions because I have. However, the frequency at which I made them was less and less and less over time. In fact, one could argue, reviewing the timeline of my life, that I potentially, based on percentage's, moved from 80% to 90% poor decision making to 10% to 20% good decisions, to better ratios over time. My reality, because I started making good decisions, became better, more harmonious, more agreeable, more successful in certain areas. Eventually that ratio changed to 50/50 in terms of percentage's, to becoming about 60/40 in my favor of making good decisions over time. Then, as more time passed and more conscious decisions were making made, that trend shifted to about 70% good decision making to 30% poor decision making. Then, I settled there because I was still not making good decisions when it came to my finances. And I was not making good decisions when it came to dating and relationships. Those two particular aspects of my life were not good and were not rendering favorable outcomes. In fact, it was not until much later down the line that I realized how poor my decision making had been when it came to money management and the quality of men I had chosen to entangle myself with, who had their own unresolved trauma's, hang-ups, triggers, projections, shadow-selves, poor thought patterns, and behavioral issues stemming from past experiences either from childhood or from past relationships which ended poorly, or perhaps both.

These are the two portions of my life pie, that did not add up. These two very vital areas of my life never made much sense because I did not make good decisions regarding relationships and money. My behavior and approach to both were juvenile, immature, ignorant in some cases, out of character in other cases, and down right, stupid. I did make some dumb decisions regarding finances by allowing an individual to manage my income taxes which snowballed into a long-term perpetual IRS problem that even now, over ten years later, I am still suffering through. Things have improved over time due to making better financial decisions, but I am still dealing with the effects and consequences of those choices. And why did make such poor decisions when it came to the men in my life and to the money I had? I am still bewildered to be honest. I joke sometimes with some of my girlfriends and say, that I think I was born or that a number of women were born with a glitch in the mind when it came to selecting a mate. Because I know I am not the only one who chose poor partners to be with. A number of my good girlfriends and I commiserate on the stupidity of our actions when it came to a particular person we chose to get involved with, only to later learn, how idiotic a choice it was to get involved with that person. We laugh about it now because we are long past those experiences, but my friends and I agree that perhaps there is a possible glitch in the mind when it comes to romance and love.

However, that is not entirely true at all. There is no glitch. There is, simply put, poor decisions which were made based upon a number of possible internal and external factors which influenced the decision in the moment it was made. In my case, I can say the influences which effected my decision making regarding the men in my life over the years had to do filling a void, of feeling codependent and needy, of needing to be needed, and not wanting to feel rejection. And where did all of that baggage come from? All of that emotional and psychological baggage came from childhood experiences, unresolved trauma's, repressed memories, crisis of identity, abandonment, abuse, a family history drug abuse and alcoholism and of other external factors, which played into these imbalanced states of mind and emotional instabilities. Of course, at the time decisions are being made to date this person or that person, I was not thinking about my "trauma's". I was thinking about how good they looked, or how much I enjoyed being intimate with them or what activity we did, or what vacation we took or what apartment we were living in or where we were moving to. I was too busy in the superficial to even notice the deeper layers of the relationship problems which crept into being about three months into each relationship, like clockwork. All of the red flags were there and, like some of my good girlfriends, I ignored them all.

However, out of those poor decisions regarding relationships, some good decisions were made in there as well. In other words, the experiences were not all poor or rendered poor outcomes, 100% of the time. On the contrary, there were some good decisions made within the confines of each relationship with yielded a good outcome, or a set of good outcomes. In other words, there were multiple silver linings around many of my dark clouds, which eventually became more meaningful and purposeful and later created the proper conditions to grow and evolve in a variety of ways and experience several profound things that came about as result of being with this person or that person. Though the relationships themselves were dying, the few vital and pivotal experiences encountered during each of my relationships were life changing and ultimately influenced the course of my life going forward in a very positive and profound way that may not have happened had it not been for making a poor decision in regard to dating this person or that person.

Conversely, I made decision, two and a half years ago, that I was done, using my relationships as stepping-stones for growth and spiritual evolution. I was done with that paradigm because that paradigm was toxic and stressful, painful and traumatizing. I no longer wanted to engage in a relationship with anyone that I felt I could "learn from". At least not in a way that was toxic and harmful. Rather, I chose to date myself and focus on what I needed and what kind of life I wanted to live. I had no more visions of this person or that, no more expectations of who I was going to date and what kind of person they should be or ought to be. All of that kind of thinking was tossed out of the window for eternity. I was done chasing my tail when it came to relationships. Similarly, I was done making poor financial decisions, ruining my credit, owing the IRS, owing debt in general, not having a savings of any kind, not having a car, not being able to get an apartment on my own if I needed to. In sum, I needed to abandon all of the old programming and old thought patterns when it came to these two impactful areas of my life and establish a new way of thinking and being.

As a result, I have improved my credit score from around 300 to about 750 in three years-time. I paid off my debts and began working on establishing good credit history so that I could finance a car, which I did, and later paid it off. I was able to acquire a nice apartment in a nice part of town. I was able to pay all of my bills at the first of the month and save a little money here and there. I even started an IRA for the first time ever. All of these good decisions kept materializing more good outcomes financially. Then of course the pandemic hit and change things a bit. But I was still able to manage myself accordingly and not fall behind on anything. I did all of these things to improve the quality of my life because I was tired of being broke, and unable to manage my life financially in the event there was an emergency. I was tired of wheeling and dealing bills each month, negotiating with companies as to when I could pay this or pay that. I was tired of being denied because my credit score was terrible. I was tired of relying on my relationships to bail me out of some financial snag that I put myself in. All of this way of living was no longer acceptable to me. Perhaps this new way of thinking was prompted because I got older. It is possible my better decision making was inspired by my aging.

Regardless of how I got to this point, I continued to keep making good decisions with regards to my finances and with regards to my love life. But as you now know, based on what I have shared, that certainly was not always the case, and I am barely experiencing a string of good decision-making outcomes. That is because the trend has been the opposite for so very long. And now I am almost fifty years of age, I am seeing the light for the first time. To be fair, it is not like good financial decision-making was not promoted in my household when I was growing up. In fact, my mother always would say to me, be sure you can support yourself. She wanted me to find a good job and stick with it, save my money, and set up a retirement account. She would always say these things to me fairly frequently. But did

I listen? Of course not. Perhaps it was her delivery. Perhaps it was the fact that I did not want a "regular" 9 to 5. Perhaps it was because I did not find the value in these concepts at age sixteen or eighteen or even thirty. Though, one could argue that by age thirty, I should have certainly found the value in financial literacy then. But I didn't. Perhaps that was because I lived the nomadic life for so long that I always managed to find my way through the financial tough spots. Consequently, those trouble spots were dire more often than not. Now, of course, I see the value in being financially literate and making good decisions with money, as the example.

Chapter 5

Glass Ceiling Theory

In this chapter we are going to explore the concept of the "glass ceiling theory" as it pertains to decision-making. But first it is worth-while to gain more clarity on what the glass ceiling theory is and how it relates to our everyday world, it's general meaning and use. For example, "the phrase 'glass ceiling' refers to an invisible barrier that prevents someone from achieving further success. It is most often used in the context of someone's age, gender, or ethnicity keeping them from advancing to a certain point in a business or when he or she cannot or will not be promoted to a higher level of position or power. Glass ceilings are most often observed in the workplace and are usually a barrier to achieving power and success equal to that of a more dominant population. An example would be a woman who has better skills, talent, and education than her male peers but is obviously being passed over for promotions."[27] Now the workplace is most certainly the most common platform for which this concept applies. However, when it comes decision-making, we can undoubtably place ourselves under the proverbial glass ceiling. We do not have to limit this concepts application by any means. We can surely apply this concept to every area of our lives and think of this concept as an opportunity to examine our life choices, our decisions, the quality of our decisions and review the outcomes of those decisions.

---

[27] Glass Ceiling Theory in Sociology: Definitions & Barriers: study.com/academy/lesson/glass-ceiling-theory-in-sociology-definition-barriers-quiz.html

Though the glass ceiling theory predominantly pertains to the workplace, let us consider the words of Patanjali when it comes to our thoughts. Because in the context of poor decision-making theory for which this book is centered, the glass ceiling theory applies as does, yogic psychology as it pertains to our thought patterns which directly influences the kinds of decisions, we do in fact make each moment of every day. For instance, according to the Sutras, "if you can have control over the thought forms and change them as you want, you are not bound by the outside world. There's nothing wrong with the world. You can make it a heaven or a hell according to your approach. That is why the entire Yoga is based on *chitta vritti nirodhah* (the restraint of the chatter of the mind). If you control your mind, you have controlled everything. Then there is nothing in this world to bind you."[28] I like to think of this passage in the Sutras as the foundation to all of Yoga. Because according to all of the Yogi's and Yogic Masters, the whole of Yoga is to understand this singular principle, that is we all have total control of the mind and that everything we experience is a manifestation of our thoughts. This is the Yogic path, which is to understand this truth. That everything which happens outside of our body and our mind, is more often than not a reflection, a creation, a result, a consequence of our own thoughts and actions.

Therefore, when I think of the glass ceiling theory, I do not only just see it as a job thing or a racial or gender inequality thing. I see it as a phenomenon which happens in life as a result of a series of poor decisions made keeping the individual locked in a redundant two step going around and around in a circle never progressing, never advancing, evolving or growing. That kind of glass ceiling, the emotional kind, the psychological kind, the spiritual kind of glass ceiling, in many ways is a lot more

---

[28] *Portion on Contemplation*, The Yoga Sutras of Patanjali, (p.6)

dangerous, a lot more detrimental, a lot more corrosive, and can cause long-term irreparable damage to one's overall state of mind, personhood, and life. In sum, the glass ceiling can be viewed as a philosophical one and or a spiritual one or psychological one. It does not have to only be viewed as a sociological one, though it's sociological meaning does lay the foundation of how our society as a whole seemingly manages to maintain a collective trajectory of social inequalities in the workforce which must be addressed. Moreover, these inequalities do not always have to dictate an absolute outcome. Though these inequalities exist in a variety of workplaces across the world, inequalities in general do not have to influence every decision which is made within the workplace for example. In fact, any injustice or inequality or disparity that one may experience in life does not have to control how one chooses to approach life or engage with others or interact with others which may be perceived as negative, aggressive, demeaning and the like.

The truth of the matter is one can certainly change their entire perspective on these kinds of matters entirely and change their entire perspective on how they see or view themselves in relation to these matters. In other words, when it comes to the outside world, we have a choice as to how to engage with it and how to navigate through it and how to create a foundation of perpetual good decision-making in one's life despite the odds presented, despite the adversity, and despite the hardships. Simply put, one can be governed by the things outside themselves, from the outside world or not. That is a choice one can make. That is a decision one can make. That is the gift of having total and absolute control over your own mind. That is the beauty of decision-making in relation to how we approach every single situation, good, bad or indifferent. Hence, "if you can have control over the thought forms and change them as you want, you are not bound by the outside world. There's nothing wrong with the world. You can make it a heaven or a hell according to your approach. That is why the entire Yoga is based on *chitta vritti nirodhah* (the restrains of the chatter of the mind). Then there is nothing in this world to bind you."[29]

I thought it would be prudent for me to repeat that passage again because sometimes the mind forgets and sometimes it is important to repeat things so that information sticks. I may repeat that passage again somewhere else in the book due to its relevancy and profundity. Similarly, I may repeat other quotes from Carl Jung and other doctors and professors to support the variety of points I am making here with regards to how our minds work in relation to making decisions, and how we experience our lives as a result of our own choices and decisions. Of course, as young people, our minds are not typically functioning at this higher level. And I say higher level, because it is a higher level of thinking. This kind of thinking is typically reserved for scribes and scholars, monks, yogis, philosophers, theologians, professors, teachers, masters, prophets, seers and mystics. This is not the kind of thinking which belongs to an eleven-year-old or a twelve-year-old, or even a sixteen, or eighteen-year-old. In fact, this kind of thinking is rarely experienced at all by a number of people as adults in this life. This kind of thinking often is regarded as too complex, too hard, too radical in some cases. Why? Because on a profound level it is complex, it is hard, and it is radical. Why? Because if you choose to raise your level of thinking you will have to also do the work required in the continuation of this evolutionary thinking. You will have to self-reflect, often, self-examine, a lot, and engage in self-analysis a fair amount of time.

Typically, not very many people wish to do that. It is all uncomfortable. Nothing about any of those things is comfortable and invites a feeling of security and warmth. On the contrary, doing the inner

---

[29] "Portion on Contemplation", *The Yoga Sutras of Patanjali*, (p.6)

work to elevate your thinking may cause you to cry, scream, yell, feel anger, fear, sadness and perhaps, after all of that, you will begin to experience a profound sense of confidence, certainty of self, and internal clarity. These are the benefits. But you have to go through the process of facing yourself head on, of dealing with your triggers, of processing in a productive manner, your emotions as they arise in any given situation that you find frustrating, uncomfortable, challenging and so forth. And that is not easy to do. However, if you do make that decision, I can guarantee you that it will be a very good decision to make that will render long-term benefits for you and those around you. The objective once you make that decision is lay the foundational groundwork, which is as the Sutras refer to as the "portion on contemplation." This is the *Yogic path to Self-Realization and Personal Freedom* as the subtitle of this book suggests.

Yet, it is vital to continue laying the groundwork here, through the reading this first part of the book pertaining to the Shadow Self, because as you begin to peel back the layers of your own consciousness, you will encounter your Shadow Self, the self that remains hidden from the world but manages to sneak out at the most in opportune times. For example, Carl Jung says that "taken in its deepest sense, the shadow is the invisible saurian tail that man still drags behind him. Carefully amputated, it becomes the healing serpent of the mysteries." [30] You may be wondering, again, what is the Shadow Self? To reiterate, according to Carl Jung, "The *shadow* archetype is composed primarily of the elements of ourselves that we consider to be negative. We do not show this side of the self to the outside world as it can be a source of anxiety or shame. The shadow may contain repressed ideas or thoughts which we do not wish to integrate into

---

[30] Carl Jung: *Archetypes and Analytical Psychology, Psychologist World*: psychologistworld.com/cognitive/carl-jung-analytical-psychology

our outward *persona*, but these must be resolved in order to achieve *individuation*. However, it may also include positive traits, such as perceived weaknesses (for example, empathy) which may not fit into the 'toughness' that a person wants to present as a part of their persona."[31] So that we have an understanding, individuation refers to one's true self. For instance, "Jung believed that by acquiring the qualities of an archetype from the collective unconscious, we repress those attributes of our true self which do not conform to the archetype. To achieve individuation and realize our true self, he claimed that, rather than repressing these traits, we must 'integrate' them by allowing them to surface from the shadow and to coexist with those in the *ego*, or true self."[32]

In other words, individuation is a process reaching full integration of owns whole mind, one's whole psyche, meeting all parts of the mind of the conscious, subconscious or unconscious and collective unconscious, thereby leaving no stone unturned in the grand scheme of achieving self-realization. However, Jung refers to the ego as the "true self". I tend to lean toward another consideration. That the true self is the embodiment of both the ego and the super ego, or higher self. Some yogis have gone further with this thinking and claim that person can reach Nirvana, which is, according to both Buddhism and Hinduism, place of peace and happiness achieved through a consistent practice of meditation. The core teachings of both Buddhism and Yogic Hinduism, of full integration of self can be experienced through, the practice of meditation and or yoga, which is the practice of contemplation through meditation and also later includes the

---

[31] Carl Jung: *Archetypes and Analytical Psychology, Psychologist World*: psychologistworld.com/cognitive/carl-jung-analytical-psychology
[32] Carl Jung: *Archetypes and Analytical Psychology, Psychologist World*: psychologistworld.com/cognitive/carl-jung-analytical-psychology

movement of the body through a series of postures and breathing techniques.

All of this to be said, that in order to gain full integration of one's true self, of one's ego and super ego or higher self, there is "work" to be done, and there are things which have to be in practice in order to begin thinking in a whole new way and that is through some kind of daily practice of some sort. But we shall get to that in later chapters. In sum, in order to get from here to there, there must be a path in front of you. But you yourself would have to create that path. And to do that, you now first realize that everything begins with you and your thoughts, how you perceive yourself, how you approach the world at large and how you process your own feelings, thoughts and emotions as they arise in response to an uncomfortable situation or when a problem persists, or when the tough choices need to be made. The glass ceiling is only a glass ceiling until it is no longer a glass ceiling. The shadow self is only the shadow self until there is light cast on the dark corners of your own consciousness to reveal all kinds of truths in an effort to reach individuation.

Now some people seek therapists for this or psychoanalysts for this kind of work. Some seek mystics and tarot readers. Some seek travel to far-away lands and study under a guru or yogi. Some start a meditation practice or yoga practice or change their diet to vegetarian or vegan or start attending lectures by high profile positive thinkers and speakers like Tony Robins. Some people simply read books to attain insight and understanding. That part is totally up to you "how" you wish to lay the groundwork to begin thinking in a more elevated way in an effort to see a life trajectory that is the result of a steady flowing stream of good decision-making, as often as you can make that possible for yourself, through the most difficult and challenging of times.

Chapter 6

Four Control Dramas

When I first read the *Celestine Prophecy* by James Redfield in 2008, I was taken on a journey into my own consciousness and how I see myself and the world at large. As result of this one book, I made the decision to read books subsequent to the *Celestine Prophecy* that incorporate the four control dramas which he introduces in the first book. What's more, the theory of the four-control drama's plays a most vital, and pivotal role in how we as human beings, potentially begin to formulate a variety of thought process, self-defense mechanisms, coping mechanisms, and ultimately, decision-making processes. However, before we dive into the four-control drama's it is imperative that I propose another consideration regarding decision-making. For instance, according to Dr. Weinschenk, in her piece, How People Make Decisions, Weinschenk asserts that "there are two different types of decisions that people make. *Value-based* decisions are made in the orbitofrontal cortex (OFC). So, during those times when you really are comparing the Honda to the Subaru when you are shopping for a car, then you are making a value-based goal decision. If Kelly was comparing the features of the different levels for the chatbot service, then she would be making a value-based goal decision."[33]

What's more, Weinschenk purports that "*Habit-based* decisions occur in the basal ganglia (deep in the brain). When you pull your usual cereal off the shelf at the grocery store and put it in your cart, that's a habit-based decision. If Kelly presses the 'Renew' button for the Chatbot

---

[33] Weinschenk, Susan, Ph.D., "How People Make Decisions", *Smash Magazine*: smashingmagazine.com/2019/02/human-decision-making

software then she is making a habit-based decision. What's interesting is that if the OFC is quiet then the habit part of the brain takes over. This means that people are either making a goal-directed decision or a habit decision, but *not* both at the same time."[34] The fascinating part about the decision-making process having two distinct nature's one being value-based and the other being habit-based, is that, based on what we have read so far, a number of us function in "habit-based" decision-making functioning most of the day. That it is only when we potentially make big financial purchases do, we really switch modes, from habit-based decision-making to value-based decision-making, which requires one to make a conscious decision to switch from one functionality of the brain to another, potentially.

Furthermore, based on this neuroscientific insight, it is clear, that we can utilize our value-based decision-making part of the brain more often and use it to our advantage. There are no rules here. No one has said to you or I that we are obligated to use our "habit-based" decision-making portion of our brain more than our "value-base" decision-making portion of our brain. No one has ever said to do that. Therefore, there are no rules to abide by when it comes to the decision-making processes of our brain which we now know occupy two regions of the brain, the *orbitofrontal cortex* and the *basal ganglia*. My question is, how do we beef up or strengthen the orbitofrontal cortex of our brain to exercise "value-based" decision-making on a regular basis? I am going to go out on a limb and suggest that it would be like exercising any other part of the body and brain for that matter. For example, I go to the gym two or three days per week and perform a variety

---

[34] Weinschenk, Susan, Ph.D., "How People Make Decisions", *Smash Magazine*. smashingmagazine.com/2019/02/human-decision-making

of heavy weight-lifting exercises to strengthen and tone my leg and core muscles.

I do this kind of weight-lifting activity to increase the power in my lower half and to manage my weight, because legs use more energy and burn more calories, therefore, my weight is more adequately managed day to day, which helps me sustain a particular weight range overall. The decision to engage in this particular regimen is a "value-based" decision. I see the long-term benefits of doing so. And just like going to the gym to work-out and grow stronger, the overall health of my brain improves as well. Similarly, I practice yoga every single day either by engaging in a series of postures and breath work or by meditation, which is still Yoga. Either way, I am doing something each and every day to improve the overall quality of my life and wellbeing. This is a "value-based" decision to do so. Because I do all of these things, my body is more flexible, stronger, balanced. Now if I can put that same kind of effort into my body, I can put that same kind of effort to how my brain functions, or how I wish to use my brain functions in terms of which regions to strengthen, such as, in this case, the *orbitofrontal cortex* for the "value-based" decision-making process.

Perhaps, because I have been thinking about our culture of poor-decision-making, I have already begun exercising that area of my brain by actively making decisions in a "value-based" manner, seeing the error of my own ways from past experiences, consistently playing out, one poor choice after another. But I also must ask, how is that many of us, perhaps most of us, seem to habitually make decisions beyond selection our cereal of choice? Being that human beings tend to be creatures of habit it makes sense that we do have a functioning region of the brain that is responsible for our "habit-based" decisions. And how has that part of the brain been influenced over the years, starting from childhood? Because in essence, in order to make a "value-based" decision, like buying a car or a home, or choosing a gym or work-out strategies, one has to use critical thinking and or divergent creative thinking skills in an effort to reach a decision. Whereas "habit-based" decision-making requires no such thing. It's almost as if, that portion of the brain is on autopilot, or cruise-control. And are autopilot and cruise-control good things when it comes to our decision-making processes? I am going to say, no it is not when we think about the amount of conditioning and programming that is involved with a "habit" pattern of thought and action. Healthy habits are good. Conversely, bad habits are bad. And in the case of perpetual poor decision-making in our society, it is clear to me that "habit-based" decisions which produce poor outcomes, are "habit-based" decisions which are rooted in negative habit patterns of thought which can be detrimental in the long run.

Circling back to the four-control dramas proposed by James Redfield, we as humans learn from our environment, which in essence is the teaching model for which we piece together our sense of identity. However, depending on our environments, parenting styles within the home, problem solving methods used within the home and overall quality of people and their thoughts, feelings, actions and words, which surround us every single moment from infancy through our developmental years, has an impact on the cultivation of our "habit-based" decision-making process, potentially. The best way to gain a clear understanding of what each control drama is, it is best to outline them here as a reference source for future needs. The four control dramas are as follows:

"1."The Intimidator"

The Intimidator is an individual who steals energy by force. In order to get an energy boost, the Intimidator may be very loud, may yell, or may use violence. Ultimately, the Intimidator gets his or her energy by forcing people to pay attention to him or her. This tactic draws more energy to the intimidator because when we are treated violently or yelled at, we cannot help but focus on the intimidator. All of this fearful focus passes our energy over to the Intimidator. This is the most aggressive of the control dramas.

Naturally, after a hostile interaction with an Intimidator, you will likely walk away feeling defeated and deflated. The Intimidator, however, feels empowered, boosted by the energy he or she has stolen from you.

2. "The Interrogator"

The Interrogator, like the Intimidator, also has an aggressive approach to stealing energy. However, the Interrogator does not rely on overt violence or intimidation, but rather uses excessive questioning and judgment in conversations. When you are around an Interrogator, you will often feel highly criticized. The Interrogator will question your decisions, your motives, and your effectiveness. This strategy, in turn, keeps you sucked into the interaction, paying attention to the Interrogator. In these interactions, you will feel the need to constantly explain yourself, and you will feel the need to justify your choices and actions. This extra attention sends your energy over to the Interrogator. After spending prolonged time with an Interrogator, you will likely feel very drained, and walk away from the conversation feeling beaten down, even though the Interrogator did not use violence against you.

3. "The Aloofs"

This one here is my personal default control drama…

Aloof people do not use a hostile or aggressive approach in their ability to siphon energy from others. Instead, Aloofs rely on being vague and distant to capture attention and energy." An Aloof is more likely to keep information from people. This, in turn, causes other people to be interested in them and approach them to "pry" information from them. It is a highly passive way of getting attention from other people. "Playing hard to get" is the game of the Aloof. An Aloof will frequently leave you feeling that he or she is playing games with you and must be chased.

4. "The Poor Me"

The Poor Me, like the Aloof, relies on a passive approach to gaining energy from others, but in a different way. Poor Me's capture our attention by making us feel guilty and responsible for them. They often complain about their problems and issues in life, but not for the sake of getting solutions. Rather, the Poor Me complains for the sole purpose of gaining our attention. When dealing with a Poor Me, we often feel like we have to "take care of" the Poor Me or we must help them in some way. We may feel we have to listen to his or her sob story over and over again, and that his or her problem is our fault somehow. This is how the Poor Me steals energy from others."[35]

Now considering that the control drama as jockeying for energy and control over another human being, it is easy to surmise that as children, our parents, God bless them, are without judgement, in a position of power and control over the child. Similarly, when we have children, we are in a position of power and control over our children. We set the rules. We set the tone. We dictate what goes and what does not. And depending on our frame of mind and way of thinking, we could potentially project our bad habits, and cyclical thought patterns and patterns of behavior and poor decision-making habits, and negative habitual thinking onto our children, thereby adding to the cultivation of their self-identity and their decision-

---

[35] "The Control Dramas"- A Lesson from *The Celestine Prophecy*, raiseyourvibrationtoday.com/2016/06/08/the-control-dramas-celestine-prophecy

making processes, self-defense mechanism, coping mechanisms, and so forth. If our attitudes are negative and our thoughts are negative and our decision-making skills have not been well cultivated during our lifetime, there is the possibility of parenting in this manner which only continues to perpetuate a particular kind of cycle unbeknown to the child, for which they absorb and therefore create a reality that reflects whatever it is they have learned in their environment, be it good or bad.

When we really think about this for a moment, this is a daunting realization to consider in the scheme of parenting. I myself am not a parent. However, I have been a stepparent at one time in my life and I was not the best suited person to play that role. It was not until I started practicing Yoga and meditation that I began to witness the plethora of negative thought patterns and negative thinking in general. As a result, I began to change the way I interacted with the children in my family at the time I was married. That said, I was a much better human to myself and to them. Hence, our relationships were much more fruitful, positive, meaningful and honest. I was able to see that parenting is well beyond just "providing" for a young person but there is a dynamic present that can either set a tone of success of that child or failure and that burden of responsibility falls squarely on the parent entirely. The hard truth is, not everyone is meant to be a parent. And I say that to those who have children in the world and have not done all that they could have done to help cultivate a pathway of personal success for the child.

Yet, on a lighter note, I tip my hat to those who get it, who understand that the responsibility is insurmountable, and that they, as the parent, or you as the parent, know that you are responsible for how your child views the world within and all around them. In sum, it is your responsibility as the parent to not project your negative thought patterns, negative behaviors, traumas and triggers onto the child or children, because the possibility of poorly developing two parts of their brain responsible for decision-making, is possible. Moreover, the "habit-based" decision-making region of the brain may potentially be used more often than the other and perhaps not so much in the most positive and productive ways. Again, these are just theories and potentialities knowing that we do in fact have two regions of the brain responsible for decision-making that need to be properly developed and that control dramas exist within each of us. Moreover, these control dramas subscribe to a set of beliefs or attitudes of each and every human being. And beliefs, be them cultural, religious, gender, etcetera are very much part pf the complex landscape of decision-making.

Chapter 7

Developmental Decision-Making

Developmental Psychology "the scientific study of how and why human beings change over the course of their life"[36] teaches us about "nature versus nurture." Moreover, "nature refers to the process of biological maturation inheritance and maturation. One of the reasons why the development of human beings is so similar is because our common specifies heredity (DNA) guides all of us through many of the same developmental changes at about the same points in our lives. Nurture refers to the impact of the environment, which involves the process of learning through experiences."[37] And according to "Learning Theory", it "describes how students receive, process, and retain knowledge during learning. Cognitive, emotional, and environmental influences, as well as prior experience, all play a part in how understanding, or a world view, is acquired or changed and knowledge and skills retained."[38] What's more, according to an article posted in "teaching and education" portion of their website at Western Governors University, there are five educational theories, cognitive learning theory, behaviorism learning theory, constructivism learning theory, humanism learning theory, and connectivism learning theory.[39]

As we continue to connect the dots regarding decision-making outcomes, I do believe that this chapter will unveil some of the hidden

---

[36] *Wikipedia*

[37] McLeod, Saul, Developmental Psychology, *Simple Psychology*; simplypsychology.org/developmental-psychology.html

[38] *Wikipedia*

[39] The five educational learning theories; wgu.edu/blog/five-educational-learning-theories2005.html#close

truths about the learning processes of a child's mind as it pertains to the cultivation of good decision-making skills, how all of this contributes to our overall identity of self, and how we as adults make decisions in which external factors additionally play a role. Because as we go through each chapter, as we learn more, gain more insights into how our brains process information, how our brains use different regions of itself to make certain kinds of decisions, and how we think and perceive of ourselves and the world around, we will, no doubt discover a new, more meaningful way to think, process information, and therefore change the trajectory of our decision-making that may have been poor, over the course of a period months and years, to reflect a consistent trend of making more favorable decisions which produce more favorable outcomes.

In an article, "What Children Can and Cannot Do in Decision Making" by Dr. Tilman Betsch, Chair of the Department of Social, Organizational and Economic Psychology at the University of Erfurt, in Germany, published in *Scientia*, Betsch asserts that "decision making is complex and requires us to perform multiple cognitive processes, such as information search, information integration, rule use, and others."[40] What's more, Betsch reports that "while children master some of these processes quite early, they spectacularly fail at others until the age of 12." Moreover, "childhood is a critical period for the development of decision-making strategies, during which children gradually become more equipped to deal with risky or uncertain situations."[41] The key point to this portion of the article is the "development of decision-making strategies" are cultivated during childhood. Which stresses my point regarding the timeline of which

---

[40] Betsch, Tilmann, Dr., "What Children Can and Cannot Do in Decision Making", *Scientia*; www.scientia.global/dr-tilmann-betsch-what-children-can-and-cannot-do-in-decision-making/
[41] Betsch, Tilmann, Dr., "What Children Can and Cannot Do in Decision Making", *Scientia*.

the decision-making process begins in childhood. Cognitively we can all agree this is the case. Therefore, when a child is developing these portions of their brain and learning from their environment, a child may rely on different decision-making strategies as Dr. Betsch has discovered during his research. For example, Dr. Betsch purports that "so far, our research has focused on children's abilities and deficits in decision making. Now, we want to concentrate on environmental factors. What should a decision look like so that children can handle it successfully? In the future, we hope to be able to advise parents and teachers on how to structure decision situations for children."[42]

Being that the focus is shifting in terms of including environmental factors regarding a child's decision-making process, one can surmise that the environmental factors are paramount pertaining to the development and cultivation of successful decision-making processes of children. Therefore, circling back to nature versus nurture, the environmental variables which include family, home life, community, friends, school, social media, as that now plays a role in a child's development, and social norms, are key aspects to how a young person perceives themselves and the world around them, particularly when it comes to events, situations and circumstances presented, thereby making a decision that reflects sound judgement, critical thinking, "value-based" decision-making, and balance between emotions and logic, because I do believe the two can cohesively coexist. That said, "the nature-nurture debate is concerned with the relative contribution that both influences make to human behavior, such as

---

[42] Betsch, Tilmann, Dr., "What Children Can and Cannot Do in Decision Making", *Scientia*, www.scientia.global/dr-tilmann-betsch-what-children-can-and-cannot-do-in-decision-making/

personality, cognitive traits, temperament and psychopathology." [43] Moreover, regarding nurture, "nurture is generally taken as the influence of external factors after conception, e.g., the product of exposure, life experiences and learning of an individual."[44] Similarly, "nurture assumes that correlations between environmental factors and psychological outcomes are caused environmentally. For example, how much parents read with their children and how well children learn to read appear to be related. Other examples include environmental stress and its effect on depression."[45]

Taking a moment to digest all of this information, let us consider for a moment that in the scheme of nature versus nurture, our environmental factors were difficult, challenging, perhaps abusive, one can surmise that these external influences have a direct impact on a child's cognitive development and decision-making processes overall. One could also surmise that these sorts of household environments can create a whole host of other social problems which a child may find themselves in more often than not, which would suggest that the choices they made were poor, thereby carving out a path of perpetual poor decision-making, creating a reality of self-induced, and self-imposed suffering. This behavior can continue well through adolescence and into adulthood, which only furthers the cycle of poor decision-making perhaps manifesting in poor relationship choices, poor money management, lack of work, job hoping, lack of stability, substance abuse served as coping mechanisms, emotional

---

[43] Nature vs. Nurture in Psychology; *Simple Psychology*; simplypsychology.org/naturevsnurture.html
[44] Nature vs. Nurture in Psychology; *Simple Psychology*; simplypsychology.org/naturevsnurture.html
[45] Nature vs. Nurture in Psychology; *Simple Psychology*; simplypsychology.org/naturevsnurture.html

instability, poor relationships with family members, inability to communicate effectively with others, inability to work productively with others, swinging from one romantic relationship to another, borrowing money, owing money, having poor credit, poor attendance at work or school, poor grades in school, the list can go on and on and on, all the while this individual is busy blaming the world for life's problems, not once questioning the source of all of it.

While I am only focusing on the negative effects of decision-making, the opposite is true as well. If a child's potential home environment and surroundings are supportive, nurturing, harmonious, stable, one in which healthy connections are made between the child and members of the family as well as with friends and healthy social bonds and attachments are formed, one can argue that the probability of good decision-making on the part of the child will be consistent. Of course, there are always exceptions to this theory. No one has the market cornered on the study of developmental decision-making. Because in science things are always changing. However, when it comes to how a child learns, it is important, I believe to support a particular way in which a child does learn, rather than to force a blanket way of learning, as each child learns differently and processes information differently. For example, according to "The five educational learning theories", "connectivism is one of the newest educational learning theories. It focuses on the idea that people learn and grow when they form connections. This can be connections with each other, or connections with their roles and obligations in their life. Hobbies, goals, and people can all be connections that influence learning. Teachers can utilize connectivism in their classroom to help students make connections to things that excite them, helping them learn. Teachers can use digital media to make good, positive connections to learning. They can help create connections and relationships with their students and with their peer groups to help students feel motivated about learning."[46]

In other words, based on this insight regarding connectivism learning, a young person or even an adult for that matter, can absorb information through establishing a connection with whom presents it. I am this way in my life. I choose particular people for particular reasons to learn from in terms of yoga, or meditation as examples. If there is something about a person that I can connect with, chances are I will learn from them. It is as if, a portal in my mind opens up for the right person. Unfortunately, growing up, I did not have that many opportunities to learn in this way and connect with others at this level for the sake of truly learning. Rather, I was learning the way I was conditioned to learn, which is the "do as I say" methodology in which both parents and teachers subscribed to during my youth. Naturally, I rebelled. I did not take kindly to the "do as I say or else" teaching and parenting method. I needed things to be explained to me. I needed to understand the reason why. I needed to find the meaning in what I was being asked to do and if it did not make sense, I would not do it.

This kind of thinking and learning method is called "Constructivism Learning Theory". For instance, "the constructivism learning theory is based on the idea that students actually create their own learning based on their previous experience. Students take what they are being taught and add it to their previous knowledge and experiences, creating a unique reality that is just for them. This learning theory focuses on learning as an active process, personal and unique for each student.

---

[46] The five educational learning theories; wgu.edu/blog/five-educational-learning-theories2005.html#close

Teachers can utilize constructivism to help understand that each student will bring their own past to the classroom every day. Teachers in constructivist classrooms act as more of a guide to helping students create their own learning and understanding. They help them create their own process and reality based on their own past. This is crucial to helping many kinds of students take their own experiences and include them in their learning."[47] All of this to be said, using my life as the subject of study in this case, my ability to learn aligned with these two kings of learning theories, which ultimately bolsters the positive decision-making processes. Because again, what we are talking about is the decision-making process, which includes learning, it includes behaviors, it includes, social bond theories, social psychology, it includes developmental psychology, and it is includes criminology at some level with regards to deviant behaviors exhibited in childhood based on several environmental factors as well as internal or genetic factors.

As adults, we now control the learning process, the way in which we process information, the way in which we choose to react and or respond to something, the way we think, the way we behave, or speak to others, our energy, our attitudes, and so on. We have total control over that. I only opted to offer the groundwork regarding the timeline of decision-making processes. We now can agree that the decision-making process begins in childhood and will either be (a) positively and constructively cultivated, or (b) negatively and destructively cultivated, both of which are entirely dependent on a child's environment. Because a child cannot work and pay rent or buy a house, put food on the table, buy clothes, pay taxes, pay bills, think about career opportunities, get married and think about

---

[47] The five educational learning theories; wgu.edu/blog/five-educational-learning-theories2005.html#close

families. These are not things children can do at ages five, six, seven and so on. A child has no control over its environment. They are at the mercy of their environment for the most part which will either be a supportive one or an unsupportive one. That is not to say, that even if one's environment was unsupportive that a child can not learn from their environment and begin cultivating good decisions as a reaction to an adverse environment. Perhaps that environment could be the reason to decide the opposite kind of environment when they are adults. We hear about these scenarios all of the time. A person grows up in a poverty-stricken neighborhood, riddled with gun violence, only to later become a CEO of a Fortune 500 Company. Clearly, they chose to start, by their own volition to cultivate a series of good financial decision-making processes so that they will never have live the way they lived when they were young, ever again, while ensuring their children will never have to want or need for anything.

Part Two —

The Awareness of Self

"Once you see what you are doing or have been doing, you
also see its futility, and that unconscious pattern then comes to
an end by itself. Awareness is the greatest agent for change."

– Eckhart Tolle

Chapter 8

Positive Psychology

Here we are. We have arrived, to part two of this book, journeying through a variety of psychosocial aspects pertaining to the decision-making processes, of developmental psychological aspects of decision-making, the yogic philosophy and psychology of decision-making, the learning theories applicable to the decision-making process as well as the neuroscientific aspects of the decision-making process. Of course, each of these aspects are merely glimpses into the world of yoga, sociology, psychology, behavioral science and neuroscience. But these are glimpses that help to sharpen our inner lens, conscious thought patterns, the conscious mind, the subconscious mind, the unconscious mind and our overall outlook on life, mental attitudes, intentions, goals, behaviors, and emotional well-being. All of these things greatly contribute to the vast landscape of who you are as a human being, interacting with others, with your reality and with your own mind. Because the truth is, our own thoughts will continue to dictate our next set of decisions we make, our next set of choices, how we approach life, how we respond to something uncomfortable, challenging, difficult, disturbing, depressing, stressful, and or life-threatening. Moreover, one thing we can probably agree, is that in life, there will be loss, there will be suffering, there will be pain and sadness. Conversely, in life there will be gains, there will the ability to thrive, there will be pleasure and happiness.

However, we certainly cannot or should not or ought not, go through life thinking and believing the worst. I have lived that way a very long time. I have entertained the "worst-case-scenario" for years. I have worried about things that have not happened for years. I have made poor decisions because I was either afraid of losing something or someone, afraid of being alone, afraid of living here or there. In fact, much of my poor decisions stemmed from low self-esteem, self-doubt, insecurity, fear, anger, resentment, pain, suffering, and more. I have held onto a variety of negative thought patterns and notions that I was not good enough for this or that, for this person or that person. I forced my way through things rather than allowing things to flow toward me for the better part of my life. I was stubborn and chose not to listen to this person or that person because I wanted to be "right", even though I knew I was wrong or that my choices were wrong or that I had the wrong information. I chose to go left when someone with sound advice advised I go right. I moved here and there, believing life would be better in Atlanta with this person, or Florida with that person, or Philadelphia for another person. There was always some emotional impetus to my moves which left me struggling to survive financially each and every move and heart-broken to boot.

My way of living, before I chose to take the leap of faith to become more self-aware, certainly is not a path I recommend for anyone. In fact, if could go back in time and speak to my eleven-year-old self, I would say, "Colette, life is going to be hard. However, if you work at making really good decisions now, perhaps life may not be as hard. Perhaps if you see the value in good decision making such as saving money, getting a bank account, building credit, focusing on education to earn the kinds of grades that will open doors for academic scholarships, work on finding a meaningful path and kind of work that will bring you happiness in life, life may not be as hard as it was for me. That is not to say life won't be tough in some areas, or that you will not experience loss or pain. But, if work on making good decisions starting now, there is a chance, you will be very successful both internally and externally." Would I have listened to myself at eleven? That's hard to answer. I think it would have depended on my delivery. Given the fact that my learning approach aligns with "connectivism learning" model, there is a strong possibility I would have taken my own advice. But we will never know because I am here now. And this is the me that I am now as a result of every single experience and choice made in my life up until this very moment. Am I happy? Yes. I am. Now.

But the search for personal freedom was not an easy pathway at first. There were a number of hard turns, bumps, pitfalls, unknown trails, twists and turns. I often felt like I did not know what I was doing or where I was going. I did the work to figure things out on my own for the most part. However, once I made the decision to take action to make the necessary changes in my life, all the books were there to aid me on my mission. I read all sorts of books including, self-help, religious, occult, metaphysical, new age, spiritual and positive psychology. In the end, they all helped the process of changing my thought process and behavior. But more work needed to be done. The work boils down to actively selecting your thoughts each and every moment of every day, which sound utterly exhausting. Admittedly, the process is exhausting at first. However, with continued persistence, patience, and determination, the amount of energy used mentally to be so selective will not be needed as much over time. Because over time, being selective in your thoughts will not require such an effort. The selectiveness will become second nature.

Yet, in the information age, the internet, social media, cell phone applications, YouTube, Netflix, Amazon Prime, Spotify, iTunes, iPads, Kindles, we have so many tools at our disposal to help us achieve pretty much anything we want and or set our minds to. Given where we are in history, there is, in my most humble opinion, no excuse to make so many poor decisions. I believe this to be more factual than not simply because, these sources are vast in and of themselves. Whatever kind of help we need, there is an app for it, or a docuseries, or a podcast or a social media groups to join. There are a number of people seeking to experience self-realization and personal freedom in one's life, that I believe it's a pretty good time to be alive right now. Essentially, the choice and decision need to be made and that will lead into the next decision. And this is where the modality of positive psychology comes into view, given how much information is out there for us to dive into at length. Because positive psychology has become trendy due to the popularity of someone like Tony Robins or others who have held events helping people to think differently. Of course, Tony Robins is just one of many people in the world who have spoken out about changing one's mindset. Positive Psychology is introduced in books like *The Secret, The Celestine Prophecy, The Seven Spiritual Laws of Success, The Power of Your Subconscious Mind*, and so many more. Positive Psychology exists in *The Yoga Sutras of Patanjali*. Even the Sutras as old as they are focus on positive psychology. Perhaps not in the exact way as it is defined but there are similarities which do exist.

Naturally, to better understand what positive psychology is, the meaning and its application will be useful in this chapter. For example, according to *Psychology Today*, "Positive psychology is a branch of psychology focused on the character strengths and behaviors that allow individuals to build a life of meaning and purpose—to move beyond surviving to flourishing. Theorists and researchers in the field have sought to identify the elements of a good life. They have also proposed and tested practices for improving life satisfaction and well-being."[48] What's more, "Positive psychology emphasizes meaning and deep satisfaction, not just on fleeting happiness. Martin Seligman, often regarded as the father of

---

[48] Positive Psychology, Psychology Today;
psychologytoday.com/us/basics/positive-psychology

positive psychology, has described multiple visions of what it means to live happily, including the Pleasant Life (Hollywood's view of happiness), the Good Life (focused on personal strengths and engagement), and the Meaningful Life. Positive psychologists have explored a range of experiences and behaviors involved in different versions of positive living, including specific positive emotions, "flow" states, and sense of meaning or purpose."[49] Moreover, "major proponents of positive psychology include psychologists Martin Seligman (who promoted the concept as president of the American Psychological Association in 1998), Christopher Peterson, and Mihaly Csikszentmihalyi. But many others have developed the subfield, and it echoes earlier work by humanistic psychologists such as Abraham Maslow, who used the term "positive psychology" in the 1950s."[50]

Thus far, the meaning and proposal of positive psychology provides a particular pathway in which one may opt to traverse. But the caveat is, one has to make a "decision" to do so. There is a choice to be made even in the engagement of exercising the basic tenets of positive psychology. Which one could argue is a good decision, which will then lead into yet another good decision, potentially? This is beginning of the beginning in essence, if you are interested at this point to start taking steps to alter the way you think going forward in terms of making good decisions and setting a trend of making good decisions or positive decisions, but it starts with making the singular choice, to do so. For example, according to *Psychology Today*, the question that is asked is, how is positive psychology applied? The article asserts that "identifying one's character strengths (such as courage, humanity, or justice) is considered an important step on the

---

[49] Positive Psychology, Psychology Today; psychologytoday.com/us/basics/positive-psychology
[50] Positive Psychology, Psychology Today; psychologytoday.com/us/basics/positive-psychology

road to the good and meaningful life envisioned by positive psychologists. There are also positive psychology practices one can try at home to promote well-being. For example, gratitude exercises have been studied by psychologists as a way to increase happiness over time. Just what the name sounds like, these involve such simple actions as writing down each day three things for which one is grateful."[51]

To further support the application of positive psychology as it pertains to better decision-making, the article, "The Art of Decision-Making" in *Psychology Today*, asserts that "the ability to think critically is key to making good decisions without succumbing to common errors or bias. This means not just going with your gut, but rather figuring out what knowledge you lack and obtaining it. When you look at all possible sources of information with an open mind, you can make an informed decision based on facts rather than intuition."[52] What's more, "decision-making usually involves a mixture of intuition and rational thinking; critical factors, including personal biases and blind spots, are often unconscious, which makes decision-making hard to fully operationalize, or get a handle on. However, there are steps to ensure that people make consistently excellent choices, including gathering as much information as possible, considering all the possible alternatives, as well as their attendant benefits and costs, and taking the time to sleep on weightier decisions."[53]

The steps in which this article suggests people take in order to make better decisions in life include the following: (1) Carefully weigh the trade-offs, commit to a decision, and then follow through on it, (2) Slow

---

[51] Positive Psychology, Psychology Today;
psychologytoday.com/us/basics/positive-psychology
[52] The Art of Decision-Making, Psychology Today;
psychologytoday.com/us/basics/decision-making
[53] The Art of Decision-Making, Psychology Today;
psychologytoday.com/us/basics/decision-making

down the decision-making process to prevent impulsive choices, (3) Gather as much information as you can, and don't allow the desires of others to dictate your decision, (4) Get enough sleep, so you can think clearly, and (5) Try to keep your priorities straight."[54] All of which seem more than reasonable if we choose to wire our thinking to reflect these five suggestions on a day-to-day basis. Which also requires us to exercise our orbitofrontal cortex responsible for our "value-based" decision-making process region of the brain, as we now know that "habit-based" decision-making is in and of itself habitual. In sum, the value-based decision-making or goal-based decision-making and the suggestions just considered to cultivate better decision-making are all ingredients to creating a more successful life in all areas of living. And success does not have to be defined as a material achievement alone. Success to you or I can be defined as being however we choose to define success as being that is relative and relevant to you or, I.

The good news to all of this is, that there are no rules. You can create the rules as you go along. You can choose the speed at which you wish to go in order to make better decisions about various areas in your life. And perhaps your decision-making process needs a little face-lift in one area or another. That is nothing to be too concerned about unless that area or areas of your life have caused you a great deal of suffering. And whatever the suffering is in your life at present, it is worth reflecting upon and consider what part have you potentially played in that suffering. Because as I mentioned in previous chapters, that theoretically, much of the suffering we experience as human beings, is largely self-imposed, self-inflected and self-perpetuated based upon the kinds of decisions we have made and choices we have made, which could have been poor in nature, potentially.

---

[54] The Art of Decision-Making, *Psychology Today*;
psychologytoday.com/us/basics/decision-making

Chapter 9

Humanistic Psychology[1]

In Chapter 8 we learned a little bit about Positive Psychology with regards to decision-making and steps one can take to potentially make better decisions. In this chapter we are going to explore aspects of its source, Humanistic Psychology, from which Positive Psychology branched out from. Because in reality, it is worthwhile to have a working knowledge or at the very least a basic understanding about some of these schools of thought in relation to our decision-making processes, personal choice, self-efficacy and self-actualization. There is no need to go too far down the rabbit hole with any of these schools of thought, however, we can collect some knowledge stones from the surface of the rabbit hole, learning what we can while we can. And if you choose to go further down the whole to collect more stones of knowledge, you of course, can do that, and I wish you well on your journey. I myself have gone down a number of rabbit holes over the course of the past fifteen plus years and I still have fun traveling down a number of new rabbit holes. In fact, writing this book is yet another kind of rabbit hole, as it is allowing me to research and read while I wrtie, which is thrilling and enjoyable. But I have digressed. Circling back to Humanistic Psychology, let us first gather a basic sense of what that is.

In a 2020 article, "What is Humanism?" written by Kendra Cherry in *Very Well Mind,* Cherry states that "Humanism is a philosophy that stresses the importance of human factors rather than looking at religious, divine or spiritual matters. Humanism is rooted in the idea that people have ethical responsibility to lead lives that are personally fulfilling while at the same time contributing to the greater good of all people."[55] Regarding Humanistic Psychology, Cherry purports that "Humanistic psychology is a perspective that emphasizes looking at the whole individual and stresses concepts such as free will, self-efficacy, and self-actualization. Rather than concentrating on dysfunction, humanistic psychology strives to help people fulfill their potential and maximize their well-being."[56] In other words, Humanistic Psychology and Positive Psychology both focus on the cup half full way of looking at an individual's behavior, thoughts, actions, feelings and emotions. While at the same time offering more holistic steps for the person to come into contact with a part of their consciousness in a sustainable, positive, and cathartic way. Both schools of thought take the more scenic road to get to the destination of self-actualization. Whereas other schools of thought focus on the cup half empty perspective, examining the individual's conditionings, trauma's, failures and in this case, poor decision-making outcomes derived from poor behavioral patterns, potentially.

One could argue that I align more with the pessimistic view of human psychology. However, I also align with the more optimistic view of human psychology. Because the truth is, the cup is both half full and half empty. There is a duality present that cannot be ignored. In sum, I cannot only focus on the positives and try to find the warm and fuzzy in everything. That is not reality. Truth is hard. Truth is not comfortable. The truth of who you are or the truth of who I am is not going to be very inviting. Understanding this fundamental reality about becoming self-aware is critical in the healing process. I would not advise anyone to try to find the

---

[55] Cherry, Kendra, "What is Humanism?", *Very Well Mind*, verywellmind.com/what-is-humanistic-psychology
[56] Cherry, Kendra, "What is Humanism?", *Very Well Mind*, verywellmind.com/what-is-humanistic-psychology

more scenic route all the time. I would advise one to accept the bumpy terrain, the hard bends in the road, the narrow and treacherous part of the path, the dark and dangerous and the uncertain. Why? Because is in the space of the unknown, uncertain, uncomfortable, that truths are hidden. They are not hidden in plain sight, in the light, in the easy, accessible areas of your mind. The truths are the shadows lurking in the dark corners of your mind, where light is lacking. The truths of your pain, your trauma, your suffering, your wounds are hiding in the deep caverns of your unconscious. That is where you must go. Think of your mind like a vast very green, very dark forest, filled with all of the elements which make a forest a forest, animals, flora, fauna, mist, peaking light from the moon, through the canopy of the trees, sounds of insects, the howling of the wild. There is where you shall roam, naked and alone through the woods, unable to see at first because the environment is so dark. But your eyes will eventually adjust to the darkness until you are able to see.

Consider this scenario as we continue forward on this journey together through these pages gaining more insight, knowledge, understanding, and clarity of vision. Because that is what I am offering through this book. I am offering you an opportunity to see more clearly, to see yourself more clearly, in hopes that you come to realize that your life script is something that you can totally control if you are willing to face the things which brought you to your knees at one time or another and embrace them like small children who need their mother or father. Because that is how you accept the totality of yourself, of the you that is you. And these psychology practices are merely tools to help you do that. These psychological perspectives are perspectives which will assist you in the process of working through your mindscape of thoughts, feelings, emotions, and more. That is what Humanistic Psychology proposes that you do, but to do it in a more forgiving manner, which I can appreciate, and I am sure you can as well. That said, Cherry claims that "one of the major strengths of humanistic psychology is that it emphasizes the role of the individual. This school of psychology gives people more credit in controlling and determining their state of mental health. It also takes environmental influences into account. Rather than focusing solely on our internal thoughts and desires, humanistic psychology also credits the environment's influence on our experiences."[57]

What I find so fascinating is the language used in the previous paragraph, with using words such as, "controlling", "determining", "environmental influences", "internal thoughts", and "mental health", because all of these words point to overall "decision-making" in the grand scheme. Why? Because one has to control one's thoughts. One has to determine their state of mental health, which requires one to take an active role in that action alone, thereby a choice and decision are made to do so. One has to focus on their "internal thoughts", which lends itself to "controlling one's thoughts", which then lends itself to making a choice and decision to focus and control thoughts in the first place. See? Each of these actions require a decision. There is a choice, an action of choice, an action to decide something, such as to "focus" which is an action, to "control" which is another action, to "determine" again, is another action. These are actions that hinge upon a choice to act at all. The alternative is do absolutely nothing. The alternative is to not act and let the chips fall where they may. The alternative is to not make any kind of decision and continue in your life as it is. And I suppose that if you are ok with that, then put the book away. We have reached the end of the line. However, if you are interested in continuing, then a decision to keep going must be made.

---

[57] Cherry, Kendra, "What is Humanism?", *Very Well Mind*;
verywellmind.com/what-is-humanistic-psychology

This is where it starts. Everything begins with a choice. Everything begins with a decision about something, at some point. Nothing in our lives is a result of not making a choice. Everything in our lives is the direct result of a choice we made, with a decision we made, including the things which we perceive and or experience as bad, or negative or terrible, or unjust. Then we have to ask ourselves, of each of those scenarios how much of those scenarios am I responsible for creating? I know. No one wants to think this way. It requires too much personal accountability and steals the blame away from the external source that you and I have been so fixed on. Because when we take personal accountability over every single situation which has occurred in our lives, be them good or not so good, amazing or utterly agonizing, enjoyable or deplorable, we have to realize at some point that we are ultimately the architect of those experiences. And going back to my percentage's theory, we humans tend to create our own misery about 80% of the time, more often than not. In some cases, some create their misery at least half of the time.

For example, according to the book section "Creating Reality", in the book *You are a Spiritual Being Having a Human Experience*, by Bob Frissell, "the basic ideas is that, as spiritual beings, it is our business to create reality. It is also our business to create what is not reality…If we live in ignorance and illusion, this is just as much our create as is living in awareness and truth. And this is the case whether we know it or not, whether we like it or not, whether we understand it or not. It doesn't matter. Reality is our creation, 100% of the time, whether we acknowledge that fact o whether we are ignorant of it or whether we deny it. The only distinction is that if we know it and acknowledge it, we have the opportunity to create reality consciously. And if we don't know it, or if we know it and don't like it or some variation thereof, we still create reality, but we do it unconsciously or in a way that puts us at the effect of life, so that we become victims having no power."[58] Similarly, Cherry states that "humanism also suggests that people possess personal agency and that they are motivated to use this free will to pursue things that will help them achieve their full potential as human beings. The need for fulfillment and personal growth is a key motivator of all behavior. People are continually looking for new ways to grow, to become better, to learn new things, and to experience psychological growth and self-actualization."[59]

You can see the trend here I imagine. There is a trend. There is a congruency with what Bob Frissell is suggesting and with what Kendra Cherry is suggesting. There is a congruency with their perspectives, with their subscriptions in terms of schools of thought, of their philosophical and psychological considerations. Though Frissell takes the more spiritual approach, and Cherry takes the psychological approach, both approaches work tandemly together to address the "whole" person regarding their feelings, thoughts, behaviors, actions, etcetera. What's more, Frissell writes that "reality itself is therefore a function of our consciousness. And that means that whenever we are facing problems or difficulties, whatever the problem might be, whether it is a personal problem, or a global or universal problem, it can only be solved by consciousness. So if it's true that we can create our reality unerringly 100% of the time without exception; and if we acknowledge this; and if we simply assert that that is true—we become, potentially, extremely powerful. We are extremely power. Yet the sorry truth is that most of us, most of the time, look at ourselves as though we had no power."[60]

---

[58] Frissell, Bob, "Creating Reality", *We are Spiritual Beings Having a Human Experience*, (p.31)
[59] Cherry, Kendra, "What is Humanism?", *Very Well Mind*, verywellmind.com/what-is-humanistic-psychology
[60] Frissell, Bob, "Creating Reality", *We are Spiritual Beings Having a Human Experience*, (p.31-32)

Between Frissell and Cherry, we have two views to consider during this journey of becoming more self-aware. And the forest analogy is just an analogy to help you to gather a sense of what it is like to unearth those truths from the fertile ground of your consciousness. The analogy is there as a reminder of what the path will be like for a little bit of time. At least that is how it felt for me for a long time. It felt like I was in a dark, heavily wooded forest, roaming alone, naked, unable to see clearly at first because it was so dark, that my eyes had trouble adjusting. I could smell the wet earth, and the moistness beneath my feet as the ground oozed between my toes. I could feel the chill in the air, as my skin re-acted and my body recoiled. I could hear the wild sounds of the night. I could feel the fear creeping up my spine, as I took each step in an unknown direction. There were times I crouched down to the ground and curled up into a fetal position on my side, feeling a kind of fright that only a child would feel in the night, hiding under the blanket, fleeing from the terrors that haunt her.

But the time came to emerge and when I did, everything changed. The decision to act and to keep moving forward was a good decision. It was a positive decision that I chose to make. Because we do have agency over our thoughts and actions, our feelings, moods, emotions, desires and so forth. We are in total control of those things and it is not up to anyone else to help us figure that out essentially. However, there is help out there if we need it. There are people, there are programs, there are practices, there are places one can go to seek the kind of help that will prove to be a benefit both in the short-term and in the long-term. And I close this chapter repeating the statement by Frissell, "reality is our creation 100% of the time."[61]

---

[61] Frissell, Bob, "Creating Reality", *We are Spiritual Beings Having a Human Experience*, (p.31)

Chapter 10

Behaviorism Psychology

Let us reestablish the meaning of this book. Because the importance of understanding regarding the title and subtitle of this book is critical, as it pertains to the decision-making process as that function relates to our consciousness. Moreover, let us incorporate the forest analogy as it pertains to the inner landscape of our consciousness as well. Now, the title of the book is "antevasin", an/te/vasin, meaning border-dweller. A yogi who has abandon the conventions of modern living to live at the edge of the forest with the other spiritual masters. These individuals traveled through the forest naked. These are the people who have left the worldly life, left the village, left the confines of conventional living to be among nature, among those who sought an awakening, who sought communion with God at a higher, a deeper level, who sought the teachings of spiritual masters, who were only interested in transcending the borders of consciousness, in an effort to experience oneness of consciousness and expansion of consciousness. That is what an antevasin is. That is who you are also. Only in this case, you are not actually going to some forest in India to dwell among other spiritual masters, naked. Of course, that is a choice to make if that will help you progress. But to that extent is not necessary. Because the journey you are on is a psychological one, it is a behavioral one, it is a spiritual one. And you only need to traverse the landscape of your consciousness in the comfort of your own home.

Moreover, the yogic path that you are on seeking self-realization and personal freedom is the choice you made to read this book. It is the action that you took to purchase it and read it. That is the decision you made to make changes in your life because you have reached a point in your mind that something needs to be done or that something needs to change, or that you are ready for something new. That is the choice you have made and that is, in and of itself, the yogic path. The yogic path is the willingness to do the mental work to change your thoughts, to realize that the mind stuff, the *chitta vritti*, is cluttering your ability to see clearly, to make sound decisions that will benefit you. And all of the various psychology schools of thought are all there to help you select the methods and tools necessary to clear out the "mind stuff" or "*chitta vritti*" as Patanjali teaches. Mind-stuff is largely the issue when it comes to making good decisions. Why? Because much of the mind-stuff has to do with conditionings, negative self-talk, negative patterns of thinking, programs (repeat ways of negative thinking imposed by the outside world through television, publications, marketing, news outlets and stories, and other mediums.), insecurity, self-doubt, and negative patterns of behavior which only reinforce more negative thought patterns.

Our mind-stuff, is the accumulative effect, from years and years and years, going back to childhood, of experiences, thoughts, etcetera. Our unconscious, subconscious and conscious minds are filled with "stuff" from the past, affecting our present and creating worry for the future. Our mind-stuff has become problematic for a number of us in our lives over the course of our lives. As a result of all of our mind-stuff, we have made all kinds of decisions, not all of which have produced favorable outcomes about 80% of the time, potentially. The yogic path is the effort of seeing that there is another way to go about living life. But first one has to accept that there actually is another way to go about living life. One has to accept that there is another possibility out there. In sum, you have to be willing to accept that there is another way to think, and "be". That you are not stuck. You are free. But freedom is in the mind. It is not a physical thing. That is the illusion. And in today's world of political polarization with "freedom" as the subject of debate, freedom must be understood as a pure psychological way of being, and a spiritual way of being, it is a consciousness, it is not about the Constitution or about Presidential Administrations or about the Bill of Rights, or about the Second Amendment, or about the First Amendment. These are all external factors which only exist in the physical domain of our lives. Though they do play a small role, they do not embody the concept of freedom that is only available in your mind.

All of that to be said, behaviorism psychology is a school of thought directly related to our behaviors and behavior patterns. However, there are layers to this school of thought. For example, according to Kendra Cherry, author of the article, "History and Concepts of Behavioral Psychology", in *Very Well Mind*, asserts that "Behaviorism, also known as behavioral psychology, is a theory of learning based on the idea that all behaviors are acquired through conditioning. Conditioning occurs through interaction with the environment. Behaviorists believe that our responses to environmental stimuli shape our actions."[62] Moreover, "strict behaviorists believe that all behaviors are the result of experience. Any person, regardless of his or her background, can be trained to act in a particular manner given the right conditioning."[63] Or in the case of poor decision-making processes, a person, regardless of his or her background, can be trained to act in a particular manner given the wrong conditioning.

---

[62] Cherry, Kendra, "History and Concepts of Behavioral Psychology", *Very Well Mind*; verywellmind.com/behavioral-psychology-4157183
[63] Cherry, Kendra, "History and Concepts of Behavioral Psychology", *Very Well Mind*; verywellmind.com/behavioral-psychology-4157183

When we consider "conditioning" as the operative function pertaining decision-making, we have to remember that conditioning can be either positive or negative, it can reflect a reward or punishment brand of training methodology or through association, and that too can reflect a positive association or a negative association. For instance, when I first rescued my gorgeous black lab puppy, I wanted his first car ride to be a fun one. So instead of driving to the veterinarian, we drove to the dog park. I let him out, and run around and sniff things, play with other small dogs, I let him be a dog and enjoy his environment. Then we drove home. The next day, we drove to the dog part again, early in the morning. I parked the car, we walked to the dog park, and he was happy to be there. He had a chance to run around, chase birds, of course, he was so small, he could only run so far and move so fast. I did this with him for about a week. What I was doing was creating a positive association with being in the car. He didn't have an accident, he did not ever get sick, he was always excited to go for a car ride. His tail would waggle, and he knew he was going somewhere. The positive association with the car allowed for every car ride over the past eight years to be a predominantly positive one. All of this to be said, according to behaviorism psychology, the mind of children, work in a similar manner.

Children will either learn from positive association or negative association. Children will either learn from a reward system or punishment system. I do believe there is a healthy balance of both. And this is where parenting styles matter as they pertain to a child's development and decision-making processes, through experiential learning. For instance, according to the Chapter "Parenting for Grit" in the best-selling book, *Grit: The Power of Passion and Perseverance*, Professor Angela Duckworth, states that "First and foremost, there's no either/or trade-ff between supportive parenting and demanding parenting. It's a common misunderstanding to think of "tough love" as a carefully struck balance between affection and respect on the one hand, and firmly enforced expectations on the other. In actuality, there's no reason you can't do both."[64] What's more, Duckworth creates a diagram of quadrants illustrating a range between supportive and unsupportive parenting as line moving vertically and undemanding and demanding as line moving horizontally, both intersecting, creating four quadrants. The top left quadrant is labeled as "permissive parenting", the top right is "wise parenting", the bottom left is labeled as "neglectful parenting" and the bottom right is "authoritarian parenting."

This quadrant is an illustration in which the reader can view the various parenting styles which may, through experiential learning, may contribute to a child's development, mentally, emotionally and through their decision-making processes. For example, Duckworth asserts that "neglectful parenting creates an especially toxic emotional climate." Keeping this in mind, as one example of how a child learns, neglectful parenting or even authoritarian parenting expressed in a negative manner, have the potential to do more psychological and emotional harm than good. And if we remember, according to the book *The Celestine Prophecy*, one of the four control dramas is the "intimidator" and there is also the "interrogator". But the "intimidator" likes to control the situation by being in charge, and through the use of fear. Such as through the use of threats, abuse, be it verbal, physical or emotional. As we can see, the toxic emotional climate for which Duckworth describes is congruent with the control drama of the "Intimidator". And from a behavioral psychology point of view, this kind of experience, for children living in this toxic emotional climate,

---

[64] Duckworth, Angela, Ph.D., "Parenting for Grit", *Grit: The Power of Passion and Perseverance*, (p. 211)

presumably experience negative association in learning and punishment system of learning.

These learning methods in a toxic environment are part of developmental psychology that punctuates how children develop, and learn behaviors, and exhibit their own decision-making. The same can be said for training dogs. How a person chooses to train their dog to be good dogs, will highly depend on how they treat their dog during the process. In other words, if you want to train your dog to not pee in the house, then you create a schedule for which you take the dog out, frequently when they are puppies, and reward them for doing their business outside. You are doing two things at once. You are creating a positive association of learning and using the reward system. The dog will eventually learn that going outside to do their business earns them a treat, therefore they will continue to repeat that behavior. Which in turn allows you to have a home free of dog urine and poop. Conversely, there is the crate training method, which has been recently frowned upon by new research that shows crate training is a subscription of negative reinforcement methods and negative association of learning, which, perpetuates the very behavior one is trying to avoid.

That said, crate training, may teach a dog to hold their urine and poop to a point that they cannot, then they go in the crate, and have to sit next to it, and are scolded for doing so. After a while, the dog will end up having more accidents and will perpetually be scolded for doing so. Fear becomes thematic in the dog's psyche. This is why I have stopped using the crate. I have kept my dog in a space that is comfortable and enclosed for him with his treats and toys and he loved his little cave. And he went out often. He never had to hold himself to the point of having an accident. I never allowed that kind of suffering to take place. As a result, he has learned on his own to hold himself because he is perfectly capable of doing so without worry. He is rewarded with treats and outdoor walks and hugged, kissed and loved. He feels this good vibration and it shows when goes for walks. The same can be said for children. Children do learn from experience and their environments. Therefore, the decisions made by children will reflect their learning methodologies imposed, and parenting styles imposed. Over time, a child becomes and adult and therefore, the adult will make decisions based on their psyche. You and I will make decisions based on how we learned to make decisions as children. Moreover, based on this proposed theory of negative association of learning and emotionally toxic climate, we, as children begin unconsciously building natural defense mechanisms, which are very much ingrained. Additionally, our behaviors may reflect a time of when we were children in many ways, even though we are grown adults. Behaviorism shows that we all learn through our environment. And if that environment is toxic, there is a strong possibility our decision-making processes will not be well balanced and positively developed.

Chapter 11

Psychosocial Psychology

In this chapter we will explore some aspects of psychosocial psychology as it pertains to the decision-making process. Because at this point, we are simply gathering all of the data so that we can gain a well-rounded understanding as to how and when decision-making develops. Interestingly, as adults we may not even consciously think about our own timeline regarding our decision-making processes or the quality of our decision-making processes. We may not even question when in our timeline did our decision-making become skewed, if it did become skewed. Of course, I had to. I had to ask myself, when in the history of Colette, did my decision-making become so poor and why did that happen, what were the factors which contributed to my trend of poor decision-making throughout childhood, adolescence, young adulthood and adulthood? Because for me, it took a long time before I started making good decisions. And even then, they were not as frequently made as they are now. Which brings me to the consideration of psychosocial psychology, which focuses on the stages of life and psychological development during each stage. For example, according to the article, "Erik Erikson's Stages of Psychosocial Development" in *Very Well Mind*, Kendra Cherry asserts that "Erikson believed that personality developed in a series of stages."[65]

According to Erikson, an ego psychologist, influenced by the work of Sigmund Freud, there are eight stages of development. "Erikson's theory described the impact of social experience across the whole lifespan. Erikson

---

[65] Cherry, Kendra, "Erik Erikson's Stages of Psychosocial Development", *Very Well Mind*, verywellmind.com/erik-eriksons-stages-of-psychosocial-development-2795740

was interested in how social interaction and relationships played a role in the development and growth of human beings."[66] This is where things get more interesting. For instance, according to Erikson's theory, during stage (1), infancy (birth to 18 months), trust or mistrust is present, stage (2), in early childhood (2 to 3 years), there is autonomy versus shame and doubt, stage (3) in preschool age (3 to 5 years), there is initiative versus guilt, during stage (4) school ages (6 to 11 years) , it is about industry versus inferiority, in stage (5) adolescence (12 to 18 years) the struggle is between identity versus role confusion, in stage (6) young adulthood (19 to 40 years), it is about intimacy versus isolation, stage (7) middle adulthood (40 to 65 years) is focused on generativity versus stagnation, stage (8) maturity (65 to death) is centered around ego integrity versus despair.[67]

"Each stage in Erikson's theory builds on the preceding stages and paves the way for following periods of development. In each stage, Erikson believed people experience a conflict that serves as a turning point in development. In Erikson's view, these conflicts are centered on either developing a psychological quality or failing to develop that quality. During these times, the potential for personal growth is high but so is the potential for failure. If people successfully deal with the conflict, they emerge from the stage with psychological strengths that will serve them well for the rest of their lives. If they fail to deal effectively with these conflicts, they may not develop the essential skills needed for a strong sense of self."[68]

---

[66] Cherry, Kendra, "Erik Erikson's Stages of Psychosocial Development", *Very Well Mind*, verywellmind.com/erik-eriksons-stages-of-psychosocial-development-2795740
[67] Cherry, Kendra, "Erik Erikson's Stages of Psychosocial Development", *Very Well Mind*, verywellmind.com/erik-eriksons-stages-of-psychosocial-development-2795740
[68] Cherry, Kendra, "Erik Erikson's Stages of Psychosocial Development", *Very Well Mind*, verywellmind.com/erik-eriksons-stages-of-psychosocial-development-2795740

With Erikson's model of understanding behavior, personality development, social development, conflict resolution in a sense, one could surmise that based his theory, the decision-making processes somewhere around school ages 6 to 11 years, will be reflective of the child's overall learning experience in the home. And based on Professor Duckworth's parenting style model, illustrating encompassing both neglectful or authoritarian parenting styles, it becomes clear that a child may not properly develop positive decision-making skills or good decision-making skills, potentially. Notably, the stage that interests me the most is stage 4, school ages 5 and 6 to 11 years, with regards to self- confidence and decision-making rooted in self-confidence. For example, Cherry purports that "the fourth psychosocial stage takes place during the early school years from approximately ages 5 to 11. Through social interactions, children begin to develop a sense of pride in their accomplishments and abilities. Children need to cope with new social and academic demands. Success leads to a sense of competence, while failure results in feelings of inferiority." [69]

What's more, "children who are encouraged and commended by parents and teachers develop a feeling of competence and belief in their skills. Those who receive little or no encouragement from parents, teachers, or peers will doubt their abilities to be successful. Successfully finding a balance at this stage of psychosocial development leads to the strength known as competence, in which children develop a belief in their abilities to handle the tasks set before them." [70] And with a supportive home

---

[69] Cherry, Kendra, "Erik Erikson's Stages of Psychosocial Development", *Very Well Mind*, verywellmind.com/erik-eriksons-stages-of-psychosocial-development-2795740
[70] Cherry, Kendra, "Erik Erikson's Stages of Psychosocial Development", *Very Well Mind*, verywellmind.com/erik-eriksons-stages-of-psychosocial-development-2795740

environment, I do believe that this sense of confidence and competence, certainly creates the conditions of a well-balanced child capable of thinking creatively and constructively, thereby making good decisions, potentially. But I am speculating. I am not 100% certain this is the case for every single child because there are genetic factors to consider. There are cultural and societal factors and educational factors to consider. Granted all of those factors apart from the genetic factors are all external factors. The genetic factors are what they are. However, the external factors are conditions in which a child will either thrive or just simply survive. Because if the conditions surrounding a child are in fact toxic, negligent, abusive, subscribing to a control drama of intimidation and or subscribing to the imbalanced authoritarian parenting style, there is a strong possibility that a child will merely survive through such conditions but will come out the other end emotionally and psychologically bruised and battered. As a result these become the traumas which are stored in the unconscious part of the mind of a child, only to later materialize in adulthood in the form potentially poor decisions, poor communication, poor relationship experiences, poor work history, poor education performance, poor family relationship experiences, etcetera.

The adult will wonder why a number of things in life do not go there way, or wonder things keep "happening" to them, or wonder why this or that person doesn't want to be with them, or why the marriage failed or why they can't keep a job or why this or why that continue to manifest. There is a culture which exists within our society which subscribes to victimhood. Not because that is what they actively choose as a mental attitude or way of living. But because this condition is unconscious. It is a by-product of a past filled with unresolved emotional issues, psychological issues, traumas, control dramas, perhaps substance abuse and any other kind of abuse, etcetera. It is an extremely difficult set of things to hurdle over when you are not fully aware of these pieces of luggage which have been carried around for years and years. Using my life as the example, for years nothing seemed to make sense or add up or last or stick or was fruitful. Most areas of my life were very stagnant up until yoga entered into my life. I fell into the victimhood of life, blaming the external aspect of life for the failures I experienced, I blamed my parents for the failures I experienced. I blamed my relationships for the failures I experienced, I blamed everyone and everything outside of myself for the failures in my life, until someone plainly stated the fact that I needed to take personal responsibility for my failures rather than blaming that which is outside of my realm of immediate control. Naturally, not everyone is ready to hear the truth. The truth as I said previously is uncomfortable. However, thanks to the learning model of connectivism, the person who delivered this message, I had a connection to, and I was able to actively listen to what he was trying to convey.

This individual had no motive, had no agenda, did not over invest or over sell the message. This individual was clear and spoke plainly and kindly. It was easy to hear what this person had to say. As a result, I took this person's advice into consideration. I deliberated for a day or two or three before I made any kind of decision, but the process of deciding on something that would change the trajectory of my life had been initiated. I switched from "habit-based" decisions to "value-based" decision-making processes in my brain. I weighed the pros and cons. I sat with the information. I factored in the evidence of a fruitful life in which this individual was living as a result of his changed mental attitude and his efforts. I thought long and hard about the course of my life and where it could potentially lead if I made the right decision, but I was also afraid of the unknown. Because once a decision like this was to be made, it would potentially alter everything. Meaning, every area of my life would be affected.

I began to worry about this and that, about my marriage at the time, about my family and what they would think, about my friends what they would think. In other words, I was worrying about the outside elements rather than considering my own judgement and abandoning the judgement of others. However, I did eventually make the decision that did change the course of my life, that did alter the trajectory, that did lead to making more good decisions centered around maturity, effective communication, patience, accountability, which contributed to more growth, more maturity, more understanding, etcetera. I was evolving slowly, inch by inch, and with every passing decision as it pertained to my mental well-being. Because at first that is all I was most concerned with. I was concerned with my mental well-being, my mental health, my emotional well-being and my emotional health. For so long both had been not well-adjusted, not well-balanced, and not well-managed. For so long, I had been emotionally erratic, and mentally unstable in some ways. One could argue that my behavior was reflective of someone who was suffering from some sort of personality disorder. And I would not entirely disagree. I was never diagnosed with that. But if I did see someone, the possibility of that being a diagnosis may not have been too far reaching of a reality given my past and given my history.

Through the practice of yoga, through Nichiren Buddhism, I was determined to do something profound for my overall state of health and well-being. I "wanted" to be a better person for myself, more than for everyone else. At that time, I could not make what I was doing about anyone else. I had to make it about myself, about my healing. Because that was all that mattered. Nothing else mattered. This decision was life or death for me. I knew that if I didn't make the choice to really try and help myself, I was going to continue living a half-life, while remaining stuck in a cyclical loop of let downs and failures, pain and suffering for which I would have been completely responsible for creating and I just couldn't do that any longer. Perhaps, some of us need to make a series of poor decisions, go through the terrible times, the struggles, the pain, the suffering, the bad relationships, the financial mishaps, the loss of money, the loss of work, the this and the that to reach a point of making a life and death decision. It's possible that for some of us, that is what it will take to get from there to here. But what I would like to say to all of that is, there is another way, a better way, and it does start when we are young. However, it can also begin right now today, by simply choosing between the life you are living right now and the life you actually want to live, consciously, completely, and with intention. But you first have to accept that victimization is present that must be addressed in an effort to become more self-aware of the triggers.

For instance, Bob Frissell asserts that "being a spiritual being having a human experience is inconsistent with what you might call a "victim mentality"—the mindset wherein we take no responsibility for who we are—for how powerful our thoughts and our feelings and our actions are…We look at ourselves as apart from other beings, and when we experience something unpleasant, we think that these other beings have "caused" it. In other words: we think we are victims…It is not true. We create reality unerringly. Period. What you think matters. It and nothing else creates the world. You are the author and the authority for your being, and for Being itself."[71] In sum, you have the ability and are more than capable of changing the course of your life by changing the way you think and therefore impacting the way in which you make decisions going forward. This is the yogic path that I have mentioned in previous chapters. It's nothing fancy, or lofty. It's plain. And simple. Yet complex, and rigorous.

---

[71] Frissell, Bob, "Victim Mentality", *You Are a Spiritual Being Having a Human Experience*, (p. 33)

Chapter 12

Humanistic Psychology[2]

As you can see by the subtitle there is an exponent of (2). That number represents part two of Humanistic Psychology because there is a particular aspect of this brand of psychology that must be highlighted as it pertains to the decision-making process. But first, allow me to introduce to you Abraham Maslow, "one of the earliest psychologists to focus attention on happy individuals and their psychological trajectory… who is most well-known for his "hierarchy of needs."[72] What is fascinating about this aspect is that it drives home a few key points about how we make decisions and why we make them according to our inner most needs. Because there are driving forces at work which prompt our decision-making processes be them favorable or poor. And Maslow's Hierarch of Needs Pyramid helps us to understand our most fundamental needs as conscious human beings. Not only was this man an optimist but he was interested in the pursuit of happiness. He was interested in growth, inspiration, aspirations, fulfillment, health, well-being and more. However, to illustrate how a person's psychological needs are driven and based on levels of importance, Maslow designed a pyramid starting with the foundational aspects first and building up from there.

For example, the pyramid contains three core sections. Within the first two bottom tiers of the pyramid consists of the first layer: *Physiological Needs*—food, water, warmth and rest. The second layer moving up a level is, *Safety Needs*—security and safety. That is the section which represents

---

[72] Abraham Maslow, *Pursuit of Happiness*: pursuit-of-happiness.org/history-of-happiness/Abraham maslow

"Basic Needs", which is pretty straight forward. The second section which represents "Psychological Needs", contains two more layers, starting with the third layer up from the "basic needs" level: *Belongingness and Love Needs*––intimate relationships and friends, followed by the fourth layer moving up: *Esteem Needs*—prestige and feeling of accomplishment. The final, top portion of the pyramid is the third section which represents, "Self-fulfilment Needs". And in this singular top layer, contains the highest level, which is: *Self-Actualization*—achieving one's full potential, including creative activities. With this pyramid there are no age ranges. That means this pyramid and the needs therein represent the human being from beginning to end. In other words, these are our needs when we are children through to our adulthood, which do not ever change. And that the course of development will always contain these needs.

Keeping these needs in mind, as they pertain to our decision-making processes, one could argue, based on Maslow's Hierarchy of Needs, that the quality of our decisions unconsciously incorporated these innate basic, psychological and physiological needs—that these needs influence our decision-making both in the "habit-based" and "value-based" decision-making processes. One could surmise, based Maslow's theory that each person seeks fulfillment, love, security, and general happiness in life, that our decisions as human beings in the world, make decisions which in some way reflect these "needs" in some form or fashion, even if those needs are distorted. For example, if I am feeling unloved and I want to feel loved and be loved, and if I have unresolved feelings of abandonment and rejection stemming from my childhood, I may, without every realizing, choose people romantically who do not have my best interests at heart. But because I am seeking to fulfill a "need" to be loved, I choose person x or person y who may, even in the short-term, exhibit a desire to love me. Similarly, if my need to feel secure and safe dictate my decision-making, I may stay in a toxic relationship in order to remain in a financially secure and safe relationship, thereby meeting my "needs".

In essence, Maslow's theory can be applied to good decisions and can be the impetus for poor decisions. This is why Carl Jung's theories and Sigmund Freud's theories matter in the larger context of consciousness regarding the conscious mind or ego, unconscious mind, the collective unconscious mind, our unresolved traumas, our shadow self, archetypes, our conditionings, our environments during our developmental years and control dramas. Though I do believe as Maslow believes that each person inherently wishes to genuinely and positively be happy, to feel happiness and to feel love and be loved. But there is the distorted tail side of this coin. Because there are those who have conditioned themselves to be happy in their misery, to be happy in their pain and seek fulfilment of more misery because the misery has become such a good friend in life, a partner in life, someone to confide in and someone to believe in. Misery has in a most insidious way, become part of the mental landscape of many people due to childhood traumas and or negative events which have cultivated a way of thinking and being. Yet, Positive Psychology and Humanistic Psychology focus on the positives of a person and the humanism of a person, through a variety of holistic therapy practices to help the individual see the positives of their own psyche and character.

Moreover, when we consider the nature of what Jung, Freud, Maslow, Erikson, Skinner and Watson all suggest regarding the mind and consciousness, how we perceive both ourselves and the world around us, through their brands of psychology, one could certainly draw the conclusion that our decision-making processes are multilayered, and not black and white. There is a lot of grey in our decision-making that many of us have not been made aware of. That is why, I find it prudent to touch on all of these various kinds of psychology practices, theories, methodologies, understandings and considerations as they all pertain to the decision-making process. It is no longer about simply critically thinking about the best car to purchase or when buying a home or deciding on what company has the better track record when it comes to investing money. Granted, those sorts of decisions are rather straight forward. However, even in those decisions the psychological layers are there, unbeknownst to this person and that person. Therefore, as you continue to peel back the layers of your own consciousness regarding the decision-making process through the timeline of your life, you may come in contact with those layers, potentially. Of course, there is strong possibility that you may not and that is ok. The fact that you are now aware that the layers exist in the decision-making process, is what matters.

Additionally, when you take into consideration your life experiences and your choices and decisions made up until this moment, as you read these words, for example, you may begin seeing a pattern in your thinking and decision-making. You may begin seeing the dots to which you now can connect with regards to various unfavorable outcomes and favorable outcomes. Because again, it is not my intention to only focus on the negative aspects of our lives and decisions which contributed to the unfavorable outcomes. It is my intention to shed light on both the negative and positive aspects of our lives and the decisions which contributed to the both the favorable and unfavorable outcomes. However, the purpose of this book is to help you connect the dots, like I am connecting the dots regarding my life and past decisions made which contributed to a string, or series or stream of unfavorable outcomes, most of which I am purely responsible for creating in my life. Very few unfavorable outcomes materialized beyond my immediate control, meaning beyond my mind and body. Conversely, much of the unfavorable outcomes are outcomes I generated due to my poor thought patterns and poor decision-making primarily attributed to past events in life, unresolved childhood traumas, unsupportive parenting styles, and poor environmental factors which adversely effected the various developmental stages of my formative years.

For example, keeping Maslow's need for "security and safety" in mind, I shall illustrate my point with one event which took place in my life, that you may find disturbing and perhaps may regard as "beyond my control", or "not my fault". But let us, for the sake of this experiment, observe the details as they are, objectively. Inserting too much emotion in to any one of these scenarios will interfere with your ability to remain as objective as you can. Case scenario number (1): In 1996, I was car jacked, sexually assaulted and shot. Now take a deep breathe because that may be a lot to digest. I know. It is. But stay with me here. Here are the facts leading up to this event. Fact number (1): The young woman I was staying with an I agreed to a suitable time limit in which to find my own apartment which was thirty days. Perfectly reasonable time frame. Fact number (2): Thirty days passed, and I did not secure an apartment. Fact number (3): My friend asked me to move out immediately. Note, she did ask me to move in as nice a way as possible, given the fact that it was a small apartment, I was sleeping on her sofa, and I over-stayed my welcome. Fact number (4): I took her request as an insult and I grew angry. And out of ego, I opted to leave in the middle of the night, thinking that by doing so would punctuate my discontent. Fact number (5): My friend did not live in the safest neighborhood in Atlanta. And I knew this. Fact number (6): I made the decision to leave at 12:30am. Which one could argue was not a very good time to move especially if I am not familiar with the neighborhood. Lastly, fact number (7): I was not thinking logically and critically about leaving in the middle of the night essentially. I was impulsive.

As a result of all of these facts, I will not define them as good or bad, but they are facts, that led to the events of being car jacked, kidnaped at gun point, sexually assaulted at gun point, then shot in the leg and robbed. The three assailants were seeking to inflict harm on someone, and that someone happened to be in that moment our paths crossed. Thankfully, I had the gumption to get up, compose myself, find help and assist the officer in finding my car, which he was able to do. Secondly, I was able to stay with a friend for a time until I was able to get back on my feet. And lastly, I learned to use a firearm which served to be a cathartic experience. But circling back to the facts, you can see objectively, that there were better decisions I could have made to avoid this level of controversy. I could have (1), opted to leave at a more suitable hour, (2), I could have waited until after I calmed down and avoid the pitfall of being impulsive, and (3), I could have not made a decision out of anger. These three things "could have", potentially, avoided the string of unfavorable outcomes for which I experienced. And this is one scenario I have time for in this chapter to share with you. But I think you can see the pattern, the chain reaction of events which led to a set of outcomes. This is the butterfly effect of decision-making either poor or good. In this case, the butterfly effect of my poor decision-making was unfavorable.

There is nothing wrong with looking into the events leading up to an outcome because when we take the time to do so, to track a timeline of choices made which led to a particular events, this helps us better understand our decisions made in the past, which then helps us fine tune our decisions made in the present in an effort to experience a steady stream of favorable outcomes based on the only things we can control, which are our thoughts, perceptions, emotions, feelings, reactions, responses, words, approach, and actions. We can control all of that, which is a blessing.

Chapter 13

Neuropsychology

In this chapter we will cover mental health as it pertains to behavior and the decision-making process, because you cannot "not" cover mental health as it pertains to behavior and the decision-making process for obvious reasons. And the obvious reasons are, when it comes to various mental health problems, behavior and the decision-making process are both influenced and impacted in a host of ways, a number of which render negative outcomes, for a number of people. That said, it is worthwhile to explore what kinds of mental health problems either do in fact affect behavior and the decision-making process or "may" affect behavior and the decision-making process. However, let us define what neuropsychology is for the sake of understanding as we continue this journey together. "Neuropsychology is a branch of psychology that is concerned with how a person's cognition and behavior are related to the brain and the rest of the nervous system. Professionals in this branch of psychology often focus on how injuries or illnesses of the brain affect cognitive and behavioral functions." [73] Moreover, "Neuropsychology aims at understanding the relationships between the brain, on the one hand, and the 'mind' and behavioral control, on the other." [74]

When it comes to behavior and the decision-making process, it is vital to understand that brain functions, in this context, matter. Why? Because mental illness is a such an important issue to include as it pertains to how the brain performs and how behavior, decision-making, emotions,

---

[73] Wikipedia

[74] Neuropsychology, *Science Direct:*
sciencedirect.com/topics/neuroscience/neuropsychology

feelings, critical thinking, are all affected. Especially given the numbers of those who suffer from mental illness in this country alone. For example, according to the National Institute of Mental Health, "mental illnesses are common in the United States. Nearly one in five U.S. adults live with a mental illness (51.5 million in 2019). Mental illnesses include many different conditions that vary in degree of severity, ranging from mild to moderate to severe. Two broad categories can be used to describe these conditions: Any Mental Illness (AMI) and Serious Mental Illness (SMI). AMI encompasses all recognized mental illnesses. SMI is a smaller and more severe subset of AMI."[75] Additionally, the terms "psychological disorder" may also be applied in this context as it pertains to behavior and the decision-making process. For instance, according to the article, "A List of Psychological Disorders" in *Very Well Mind*, Kendra Cherry states that "the term psychological disorder is sometimes used to refer to what is more frequently known as mental disorders or psychiatric disorders. Mental disorders are patterns of behavioral or psychological symptoms that impact multiple areas of life. These disorders create distress for the person experiencing these symptoms."[76] We also have to include substance abuse and addiction.

Taking a short breath here to digest that bit of information, you can surmise, more than likely, that if people experience "any mental illness" or "severe mental illness" or a "psychological disorder" or even "addiction" of some substance or behavior, which happens to involve over 50 million American's, "good decision-making" in this context is questionable. If regions of the brain responsible for the decision-making process are

---

[75] Mental Illness, *National Institute of Mental Health*:
nimh.nih.gov/health/statistics/mental-illness
[76] Cherry, Kendra, "A List of Psychological Disorders", *Very Well Mind*:
verywellmind.com/a-list-of-psychological-disorders-2794776

impaired due to any one mental illness or psychological disorder or addiction, it stands to reason that the probability of making more poor decisions than good decisions is much higher, potentially. Neurochemically, our brain chemicals such as dopamine, norepinephrine, serotonin, glutamate, GABA and acetylcholine are designed to be in balance with one another, creating the conditions for good cognitive performance of the brain. And just so we are clear about what cognitive function is, "cognition is defined as 'the mental action or process of acquiring knowledge and understanding through thought, experience, and the senses. It is in essence, the ability to perceive and react, process and understand, store and retrieve information, make decisions and produce appropriate responses."[77] Therefore, when our brain chemicals are out of balance, our cognitive function is not at its best.

Now there is a pretty hefty list I will refer to here, but I do not want to overwhelm you with all of the details in this list. So, I will share some of the major mental health issues that many Americans experience every day, which, for the sake of this book, interfere with one's decision-making process and behavior overall. For instance, according to the article, "A List of Psychological Disorders" in *Very Well Mind*, there are fifteen main disorders with a subset of disorders for each. But I will provide some of disorders and subsets the to keep things relatively brief. The psychological disorders include the following:

1. *Neurodevelopmental Disorders*, which include things like Autism Spectrum Disorder and Attention-Deficit Hyperactivity Disorder.

2. *Bipolar and Related Disorders*, which include things like mania and depressive episodes.

---

[77] "What is Cognition", *Cambridge Cognition*:
cambridgecognition.com/blog/entry/what-is-cognition

3. *Anxiety Disorders*, which include things like generalized anxiety disorder, social anxiety disorder, and panic disorder.

4. *Stress-Related Disorders*, which include things like acute stress disorder and post-traumatic stress disorder.

5. *Sleeping Disorders*, which include things like such as insomnia disorder and narcolepsy.

6. *Disruptive Disorders*, which include things like intermittent explosive disorder and conduct disorder

7. *Depressive Disorders*, which include things like major depressive disorder and persistent depressive disorder.

8. *Substance-Related Disorders*, which include alcohol- related disorders, I will add (pharmaceutical-related disorders, as opioid addiction has soared in this country over the past decade.), stimulant use disorder, and tobacco use disorder, gambling, sex and pornography.

9. *Personality Disorders*, which include things like anti-social personality disorder, narcissistic personality disorder, and borderline personality disorder.

10. *Neurocognitive Disorders* which include things like Alzheimer's, Parkinson's Disease, Dementia and Delirium.

11. *Schizophrenia*

12. *Eating Disorder*

13. *Obsessive Compulsive Disorder*

14. *Somatic Symptom Disorder*

15. *Dissociative Disorder*[78]

---

[78] Cherry, Kendra, "A List of Psychological Disorders", *Very Well Mind*: verywellmind.com/a-list-of-psychological-disorders-2794776

The list is helpful when we stop to consider how these disorders which plague so many, and that is not a judgement but a fact, may affect people's behavior and decision-making process. But I am not a doctor. I cannot say with absolute certainty that these disorders do impair judgement, the decision-making process and behavior. However, given all that we have learned so far, we can certainly surmise that the decision-making process and behavior are impacted in some kind of way. And that is why the field of neuropsychology exists. Because mental health and behavior are locked in a two-step, dancing from one end of the dance floor of life to the other. And that two-step is not the most graceful of movement. Therefore, to reiterate, "Neuropsychology is the discipline which investigates the relations between brain processes and mechanisms on one hand, and cognition and behavioral control on the other."[79] For example, according to the article "The Neuroscience of Making a Decision" in *Psychology Today*, Christopher Bergland asserts that "decision-making is in the locus of your control. You have the power to break patterns of behavior simply by making better decisions. You can change your mind and your actions at any time. Even when you're stuck in a cycle of rut-like thinking and behavior, a change of attitude and decision-making can turn your life around."[80]

Of course, what Bergland is suggesting when he says, "you have the power to break patterns of behavior simply by making better decisions", which is a lot easier said than done, is, seek the medical help that you may need to first address whatever mental health concerns you may have. Seeking proper medical attention is a critical first step, and that is the start

---

[79] Neuropsychology, *Science Direct*: sciencedirect.com/topics/neuroscience/neuropsychology
[80] Bergland, Christopher, "The Neuroscience of Making a Decision", Psychology Today: psychologytoday.com/us/blog/the-athletes-way/201505/the-neuroscience-making-decision

of "good decision-making". We do not always want to acknowledge that there is problem because mental health is still a taboo subject in our culture and therefore, denialism is at the center of our decision-making to a large extend which then leads to poor or unfavorable outcomes, more than likely. Hence the likelihood of poor decision-making is strong for those who "think" there is a mental health concern and do not seek help and continue on with life, business as usual, thinking it will work itself out. Unfortunately, when mental illness is present and is untreated, the mental illness will persist and progress, thereby continually influencing every single decision made, every thought, every behavior, feeling, mood and emotion. There is no escaping this or sweeping it under the rug. There is only accepting what is, seeking help, and making a plan to follow each day to put you on a positive path toward recovery and wellness.

Recovery is key to better cognitive performance and functionality. Recovery is vital in the scheme and scope of better decision-making, self-control, focus, and self-discipline, all of which support feelings of security, personal agency and efficacy, feelings of confidence, self-reliance, and an overall sense of health and wellbeing in every area of your life. In fact, when you are better, everyone else around you are better. When you are not at your best, everyone else is not at their best. Therefore, it is of the upmost importance to subscribe to "self-care" in this context, which will render long-term benefits for years and years to come. Everything in your life essentially improves, as a result of self-care efforts to support your state of mental health. Because if your state of mental health deteriorates over time, your decision-making process will likewise deteriorate. What's more, when you take the time to meet yourself where you are, mentally, you seize the opportunity to make a difference in your own life for the better. I guarantee that you do. Your consistent and persistent efforts to improve your state of mental health will by the sheer law of cause and effect, will enhance the quality of your life in general.

You may be wondering if I sought the help that I needed to address my mental health issues. Admittedly, I did not. And because I did not want to, but because I did not realize I had mental health problems until I started writing and reviewing my life. Now I did know about the Attention-Deficit Hyperactivity Disorder. That I was diagnosed with when I was about seven or eight years old. And at the time, my mother was told that I needed to be on Methylphenidate also known as Ritalin. She declined. I think she felt at the time that this particular pharmaceutical would be more damaging in some way or another, than to not take it. But I wonder if she made the right decision in that moment, given my history of behavioral issues, aggression, violent mood swings, poor decision-making, emotional outbursts, fits, tantrums, and other unsavory theatrics and behaviors. I do remember attending family counseling for a short time. But that didn't take. In other words, I really did need help as a young person to help me get my brain chemistry in order. Not having medication may have caused more harm than good during early childhood and adolescence. As an adult, I could have benefited from some low dose of something to help with my anxiety, depression, compulsiveness, emotional instability and irrationality. I truly needed help. And eventually the help came, but in the form of meditation and yoga, herbs and other plant-medicine.

At the time I started practicing Buddhism, I was running low on moral and felt a profound feeling of despair and harbored thoughts of suicide at a particular time in my marriage. I was unable to conceive a child which only added to the depression, anxiety and feelings of loneliness. I didn't know what to do. No one said, hey, I think you should get help. And even if they did, I would not have known where to begin. Instead, a family member suggested I start practicing Buddhism as a possible solution to my problems at the time. I gave it a try because nothing else was working. But, I made a "decision" to "try". That decision changed the course of my life. That one decision to try, led to another decision to enroll in a 200 Hour Yoga Teacher Training Program. And that decision led to another decision to learn about Foot Reflexology. Which then led to the decision of learning Reiki. Each decision made space for yet another kind of decision. Amid these decisions, I decided to read books about *Courage, Compassion, Intuition, Intimacy, Freedom* (all of which were written by Osho), *The Art of Practical Spirituality*, the *Seven Laws of Success, The Pilgrimage, The Alchemist, The Power of the Subconscious Mind, The Alchemy of the Hear*t and so many other books during my yoga teacher training. This was my therapy. This was how I began to change the tide of my life. Though it was not easy. The work I have done took years and years. And I still had more work to do. Fast forward, from 2004 to 2017, I engaged in three Ayahuasca Plant-Medicine Rituals/Ceremonies. As a result of doing so, my brain chemistry was corrected to such a degree that I am more focused, able to sit and write books, emotionally balanced, able to critically think about this and that.

In other words, all of the choices made—all of the decisions made which then led to dating a person involved in plant-medicine, allowed me to engage with Mother medicine as it is referred. These experiences made me a better me. In fact, I wrote a book about it, called *The Miracle of Plant Medicine and the Practice of Yoga* in 2018. And now I am in community college, pursuing a degree in sociology, currently earning a 4.0, which given my past, is remarkable. My brain is better, I'm better, my life is better because of all of the life changes made over the past fifteen plus years. That is not to say, I still do not have my moments. I do. I am triggered like everyone else. But I have years of practice to now rely on to help get myself back on track. And I am not alone. I have an excellent support-system, I have people in my life who care about me and support me. I have a community filled with people who look out for one another. And I have my faith and trust in God, the Universe, in life, that everything in the end will be ok. But I have to allow myself to "feel" my way through things and provide myself "space" to just be present with what I am feeling and the "room" to work things through at a pace that is comfortable, manageable and sustainable. I also talk to my significant other to keep him in the loop. We communicate as effectively as we can to work through either his moments of this or that or my moments of this or that. As a result, we work together as a team, which is most important.

I will close this chapter, which ran a little longer than all of the other chapter thus far, by saying, though this is the path that I chose, does not mean it is a path for everyone. But, aspects of my path are for everyone, such as meditation, yoga, self-reflection, understanding our mental landscape/ consciousness, observing our thoughts, being mindful of our thoughts, contemplating our thoughts, or just being in a state of contemplation and of observing oneself and the world at large. Moreover, deferring to various breathing techniques, and mindfulness exercises are incredibly useful. Similarly, establishing a consistent and persistent meditation practice is definitely going to be one of the most beneficial tools that will in fact, help your brain be a better brain. And will help you be a better you. I can testify to that. Because before plant medicine even came into the picture, my meditation practice was and still is what guides me each and every day. Period. Then everything else is included as tools and means to manage my emotions, feelings, thoughts, etcetera. In sum, meditation is worth considering.

Chapter 14

Yogic Psychology

Here we are in the last chapter of part two of this book. Hopefully, you have gained a variety of insights, perspectives, and information about the decision-making process thus far. Of course, we still have part three to guide us through to the completion of this book. But I am excited that you stuck with this so far. I think that by making the attempt to learn something new is a giant leap forward in your journey, as it is in mine, to be honest. Writing this book and sifting through memories, looking at the timeline of my own life has been a roller coaster ride. Moreover, this book has been very quickly written in the wake of my father's passing a week before I sat down to write. I suppose the book was already written in a way. That by the time I sat down and put my fingers on the keys of my laptop, the book was writing itself. This is when I know I am in the flow of something amazing. Because when effortlessness of something rides tandemly next to doing the work and being proactive to get things done, things flow. When my mind is clear and focused, I achieve so much in such little time. But much of this way of operating is attributed to all of the work put in to enhancing the quality of my mental state, my health and wellbeing, and my life in general. And as I stated in the previous chapter, meditation was the thing that helped get me from there to here.

In this chapter we are going to dive into "yogic psychology" which is not actually regarded as a branch of psychology in the United States but is regarded in academia as a branch of psychology in the United Kingdom. Moreover, yogic psychology or yoga psychology, though not held in the same regard as positive psychology or humanistic psychology, yogic psychology through the teachings of Patanjali is a way to address the mind, mental states, and how to understand them, how to work through them, how to best engage with the mental sphere through meditation and contemplation. In truth, yogic psychology, should be highly regarded in this country given the fact that over 300 million people practice yoga worldwide and over 37 million people practice yoga in the United States.[81] In fact, "the number of yoga practitioners in the United States has almost doubled in the past decade, according to yoga statistics in America. Now, 1 in 10 Americans practices yoga, making the United States one of the top countries where the discipline is practiced. According to yoga statistics in the UK, there are over 10,000 yoga masters in the UK who teach over 460,000 British yogis every week. The interest in yoga in the UK rises by 73% every year."[82]

There is a clear interest in the practice of yoga that these figures illustrate. Furthermore, with every passing year, the numbers of people who practice yoga increase, which suggests that people are finding the value in practicing yoga for a whole host of reasons. The most valued reasons hare centered around mental health, mental wellbeing, emotional wellbeing, and psychological health and wellbeing overall. For instance, "research has shown that spending just 15 minutes practicing yoga every day can make positive changes to the brain's chemistry, increase your emotional stability, and improve your mood."[83] These are some of the neuroscientific aspects we are considering. This chapter will dive a deeper into this brand of

---

[81] Hrubenja, Alexander, "Yoga Statistics and Facts: 2021 Edition", *Modern Gentlemen*: moderngentlemen.net/yoga-statistics/
[82] Hrubenja, Alexander, "Yoga Statistics and Facts: 2021 Edition", *Modern Gentlemen*: moderngentlemen.net/yoga-statistics/
[83] Hrubenja, Alexander, "Yoga Statistics and Facts: 2021 Edition", *Modern Gentlemen*: moderngentlemen.net/yoga-statistics/

psychology. For example, according to *The Yoga Sutras of Patanjali*, Sri Swami Satchidananda asserts that "for the keen student this one Sutra (the restraint of the modifications of the mind-stuff is Yoga), would be enough because the rest of them only explain this one. If the restraint of the mental modifications is achieved one has reached the goal of Yoga. The entire science of Yoga is based on this. Patanjali has given the definition of Yoga and at the same time the practice. "If you can control the rising of the mind into ripples, you will experience Yoga.""[84] You may be wondering again, what Patanjali means when he says "mind-stuff". I wondered this as well when I began my yogic training. And even then, I was left bewildered. My mental understanding was not seemingly big enough to comprehend the meaning at the time. However, there is a simpler way to understand the meaning.

In sum, mind-stuff simply means all of the mental chatter, all of your thoughts of the past and future, all of your projections, past histories, past traumas, past emotional baggage, fears and worries, anger, resentments, pain, sufferings, insecurities, triggers, negative thought patterns, cyclical thought patterns, feelings (positive and negative), emotions (positive and negative), archetypes (as we discussed in previous chapters), shadow self (as discussed in previous chapters), wounds, etcetera. These are all what constitutes as being "mind-stuff". So, you can see how much "mind-stuff" we all have. That is why in *The Yoga Sutras of Patanjali*, the first book of the four, is the "Portion on Contemplation". This is the most important book of all four which defines Yoga, which gives Yoga its meaning and its purpose. It gives Yoga its mission and practice. It is not about postures and breathing practices per say. Though these two aspects do become a part of one's physical and emotional journey, they are only

---

[84] Portion on Contemplation, *The Yoga Sutras of Patanjali*, (p. 3-4)

"aspects"—two limbs of an entire Eight Limbs of Yoga. Therefore, when you read the "Portion on Contemplation", you must read each paragraph slowly, allowing time and space to think about the content and how it actually applies to your life in real time.

However, for the sake of this book, I will do my best to simplify some of these concepts in an effort to maintain contextual clarity in an effort to establish a link between yogic psychology and the decision-making process. For example, in a previous chapter I introduced the concept of "mind-stuff" as it pertains to behavior and the decision-making process. Moreover, I discussed how our thoughts govern our experiences and our reality. For instance, Sri Swami Satchidananda states that "the entire world is based on your thoughts and mental attitude. The entire world is your own projection. Your values may change with a fraction of a second. Today you may not even want to see the one who was your sweet honey yesterday. If we remember that, we won't put so much stress on outward things. That is why Yoga does not bother much about changing the outside world. There is a Sanskrit saying…as the mind, so the man; bondage or liberation are in your own mind." If you feel bound, you are bound. If you feel liberated, you are liberated. Things outside neither bind nor liberate you; only your attitude toward them does that." [85]

Now, one could argue, that all of this is easier said than done. And I would not entirely disagree. Because it is always going to be easier said than done. That is why the Sutras provide steps in order for one to come to this realization in their own lives and all of the mental and emotional challenges presented. Patanjali is not saying to disregard your mental health concerns but rather to understand, that even in mental health, our thoughts have an impact on our experiences and our reality. That even with mental

---

[85] "Portion on Contemplation", *The Yoga Sutras of Patanjali*, (p.5)

health problems, our thoughts and our behavior have an effect on our external environment. And that in knowing that, perhaps, you may begin to see just how powerful your thoughts truly are and how you have the power to liberate yourself from even yourself. Simply put, our thoughts can either create a hell or heaven for us. That your thoughts can create a hell or a heaven for you. That your thoughts can either keep you in bondage or liberate you. So, when people seek to become "liberated" by going to some yoga retreat for example, (which is always a nice thing to do), or travel to some remote part of the world staying at an ashram (which is always a nice thing to do), or to study with a guru (which, again, is always a nice thing to do), or attend an Ayahuasca ceremony (which, is always going to be a nice thing to do), they are not fully understanding that the concept and the process of liberation will not ever come from these external sources. Not ever. Perhaps, they will inspire something in you. Perhaps, these external experiences will inspire a thought which then will be the impetus for a series of other kinds of thoughts that are positive and position you to travel internally in a positive direction. And perhaps, these external experiences will prompt you to consider something that you might not have otherwise considered had you not gone to India or Sedona, or Peru.

The point to the traveling and the ashrams and ceremonies is to inspire you to do something, to take action, to consider something positive and impactful. That is all. You are to take those inspirations and use them to help *you*. But at the end of the day, you have to do the work each and every day to improve your state of mental health and wellbeing. You have to do the work to improve the quality of your mood, your feelings and your emotions. And that daily effort, is arduous but well worth the effort in general for the benefit your efforts will bring you over the course of your life. That is how good decision-making is triggered. And that is how your life course will be altered as a result of the series of good decisions you make because you are doing things each and every day to manage your mental sphere and everything which is contained within it. That is what Patanjali is trying to convey and that is what the "Portion on Contemplation" is all about. Moreover, Patanjali provides actions to take to continue on your journey of contemplation. Because contemplation is a daily mental activity. Of course, you can probably download some apps to your phone to help you track this effort. Because there's an app for everything just about. For example, there is an app called "Headspace" you can download to your phone and pay for a monthly subscription if you are interested in accessing all this application has to offer. I did. I love it. It is one of the greatest tools I have at my disposal. This did not exist in 2005. If it did, I would have used it religiously.

My point here is to illustrate the fact that applications like "Headspace" are designed to help you connect with other likeminded people because it is another social media platform, and you can engage in a wide variety of meditations. Honestly, I could go on raving about this application, but I am confident you understand that there are all sorts of tools to help you either start or maintain a meditation practice centered around mindfulness and contemplation. That is the beauty of being alive right now. That we have access to these kinds of tools and applications to be there for us and help us along, in addition to the books that we may read or the documentaries that we may watch about Yoga, or Yogic Psychology, Philosophy, Practice and more. Though these modern inventions did not exist 5,000 plus years ago, the intention behind them are aligned with a 5,000 plus year old system and science of being. And simply making the decision to download an application to your android or iPhone is a good decision. Which means that you are taking control over your thoughts at the smallest level which will later encompass an entire swath of your life and conscious state of being.

For example, Sri Swami Satchidananda states that "if you can have control over the thought forms and change them as you want, you are not bound by the outside world. There's nothing wrong with the world. You can make it a heaven or a hell according to your approach. That is why the entire Yoga is based on *chitta vritti nirodhah* (the restraint of the modifications of the mind-stuff is Yoga). If you control your mind, you have controlled everything. Then there is nothing in this world to bind you."[86] Furthermore, when you are ready, Patanjali continues to share about the ways in which you can have better control over your mind, over your thoughts, moods, feelings and emotions, with the following Sutras. For instance, the third Sutra talks about the fact that you are the "Seer". According to Sri Swami Satchidananda, "you are that true Seer. You are not the body nor the mind. You are the Knower or Seer. You always see your mind and body acting in front of you. You know that the mind creates thoughts; it distinguishes; otherwise, it seems to distort the truth."[87] In other words, you are an Observer. That you are also this observer, a seer, one of "higher" mind to see the truth of who you are, of your thoughts and of your body, as if looking into a mirror and seeing the true reflection of who you are, but then when the negative thoughts occur, they distort the perfect most beautiful image, that is You. It is like seeing your reflection in a calm still body of water, without any ripples.

For example, Satchidananda claims that "to see the true reflection, see that the water is clean and calm and without any ripples. When the mind ceases to create thought forms or when the *chittam* (mind) is completely free from *vrittis* (stuff), it becomes as clear as a still lake and you can see your true Self… by making the mind clean and pure, you feel you have gone

---

[86] "Portion on Contemplation", *The Yoga Sutras of Patanjali*, (p.6)
[87] "Portion on Contemplation", *The Yoga Sutras of Patanjali*, (p.6)

back or you appear to have gone back to your original state."[88] Put another way, by doing the work to clear your mind, to empty out all of the stuff that cause you suffering, or that generates cyclical thought patterns that put you in mental grid lock, thereby perpetuating poor decisions, causing you more suffering and stress, anxiety, sleeplessness, etcetera, you ultimately begin to see Yourself more clearly. That you begin to feel lighter, less weighed down, happier, more in tune with others in a positive way, more in tune with yourself in a positive way. You begin to experience a profound feeling of calm and mental clarity that was not there before. So, by taking time out each day to reflect, contemplate, in a seated manner of some sort comfortable for your legs and body, to breathe and just simply be right where you are, there is this possibility. And that small window of opportunity will grow wider and last longer, until you can experience your life as the Seer on a day-to-day basis, which is infused with every thought and every decision made.

This is the Yogic Psychology in which *The Yoga Sutras* offer. *The Yoga Sutras*, in *Book One*, the "Portion on Contemplation" is the foundation of Yoga and how we as human beings can come into contact with our true nature, beyond the noise, the drama, thoughts, and everything else. Because when all of those things are sorted out, worked through, solved, and let go of, the person that you wish to become is right there within you, present and available. Perhaps, the yogic postures help get you there, or seated meditation gets you there, or the combination of both practiced each and every day, help to get you there. But the effort comes from your daily commitment to yourself, to your self-care as we touched on before, to your physical and mental health and wellbeing.

---

[88] "Portion on Contemplation", *The Yoga Sutras of Patanjali*, (p.7)

Part Three —

The Realized Self

"Drop the idea of becoming someone, because you are
already a masterpiece. You cannot be improved. You have only
to come to it, to know it, to realize it."

– Osho

Chapter 15

GRIT Theory

Over the course of, twenty-two years or so, I have lived in different cities in this country. For example, in 1996, I made a seemingly snap decision to move to Atlanta after only visiting it once in my life. I was accepted to attend Clark Atlanta University. Which was pretty amazing when I think about it. So, I packed up my car and with the company of a friend, I drove 3,000 miles straight to Atlanta to start my new life. Sadly, the college plan did not stick due to my car-jacking incident. Naturally, I used it as an excuse to not commit to the plan. Instead, I got a job at the Cheesecake Factory and job hopped for a while, never settling on one thing, but met a lot of interesting people, cultivated a variety of job skills and had the chance to work in the record business when Atlanta was the epicenter, and home for many rappers and hip-hop artists such as CeeLo Green, and Outkast, musicians, bands, r&b artists like TLC, Boyz II Men, P!nk and more. As a result, I met someone, then met someone else, then eventually moved to Mount Vernon, New York, just a short train ride from Manhattan, in 1999.

I later married, moved back to Atlanta with my husband at the time, which did not work out, then moved to a quiet suburb on the Long Island Sound, called East Norwalk, Connecticut in 2003. It was a beautiful place. We rented the bottom floor of an old two-family Victorian home. We had two Rhodesian Ridgebacks, that went with us during our Appalachian Trial camping trips, kayaking trips, boating excursions, and family trips to Atlanta. During my time in Connecticut when I thought my life was falling apart, I was prompted to practice Nichiren Buddhism, which led to the decision to take up yoga in 2005. I started a training program in January and graduated in June and started teaching Yoga. Prior to that I was a Special Education Assistant Teacher for Norwalk Public Schools, which was rewarding but I did not have a degree to pursue anything further with a better salary. But I wanted to help people and I wanted to be in a teaching capacity. So, Yoga was it. And it stuck. The marriage did not. And I moved back to Atlanta in 2007. There is where I began my teaching career, teaching at a variety of studios and working privately with clients. I did this for five years. I met someone who was from St. Pete, Florida, who had to move back to Florida, and after losing a dog, I decided to move to Florida as well, in 2012. Within a year of living in St. Pete, I opened my own yoga studio, called Wild Lotus Yoga Studio, which was the most amazing local community studio ever. I am biased. I can say that. It was magical. During my time in Florida, I trained to be a personal trainer and got certified. I learned to grow cannabis, I learned about cannabis culture. And I learned about psychedelics and plant medicine, for which I engaged.

I met someone for that and then met someone else after that, which later led to moving to Philadelphia in 20017. Though relationship did not stick, my commitment to my craft remained. I began teaching at a variety of local yoga studios such as Philly Power Yoga and The Sporting Club at the Bellevue, while also building client relationships to teach yoga privately. During my time here so far, I made a commitment to go back to college and earn my undergraduate degree, starting out at Community College of Philadelphia and eventually transfer to Temple University. But, the most interesting aspect of my time here, is during my time teaching at Philly Power Yoga, I met Angela Duckworth. She was a yoga student in my class, and I had no idea "who" she was. To me, she was an awesome person who always enjoyed taking class and attending my class. I appreciated her consistently showing up for my yoga classes on a Saturday afternoon. We would intermittently chat on her way in and out. After about a year, another yoga student brought to my attention "who" she was. Moreover, I was fortunate to have had the chance to speak with her about my educational goals and to help me sort out which direction would be best to take. I was also fortunate to have read her book GRIT. I wanted to know more about her as a person and her work. So, here we are. This will be the time to briefly talk about GRIT.

I shared with you, my travels of where I moved, what I did in each place I lived more or less, to use those experiences as examples regarding GRIT as it pertains to my behavior and decision-making process. For example, according to *GRIT, The Power of Passion and Perseverance*, Angela Duckworth asserts that "it's often said that the last mile is the longest. Grit keeps you on the path."[89] Duckworth also suggests that grit is not the only means of success in life. "A lot of factors determine success. Emotional intelligence. Physical talent. Intelligence. Conscientiousness. Self-control. Imagination. The list goes on…Because grit holds a special significance for the achievement of excellence. This is true whether the endeavor in question is physical, mental, entrepreneurial, civic, or artistic. When you look at the best of the best across domains, the combination of passion and perseverance sustained over a long term is a common denominator."[90]

You may be asking what does this perspective have to do with the decision-making process or behavior? When you stop and think about what Grit implies at its core, is gumption, guts, and "gritiness" as she calls it to make a commitment to yourself and see it through to its completion. This way of thinking can be useful when you consider your decision-making processes, your desire to improve the quality of your life, your gumption

---

[89] Duckworth, Angela, *GRIT: The Power of Passion and Perseverance*, (p. 291)
[90] Duckworth, Angela, *GRIT: The Power of Passion and Perseverance*, (p. 291)

and guts and "grittiness" to do everything that you can to sustain a commitment to yourself to be a better version of yourself, to change your life course, simply by choosing something different for yourself, something that is positive, constructive, long lasting, meaningful, purposeful, healthy, sustainable, and beneficial. Adopting the Grit theory that when you make a commitment to yourself you dig into the core of your being and do the work and achieve your goals, the short-term goals and the long-term goals rooted in good decision-making, without judgement and without looking back on the past. Because at this point, there is only, looking forward, moving forward, taking each step forward in a direction that will enhance both the quality of your life and the quality of your mind, your mental sphere, your consciousness, your ability to think critically, thoughtfully, and intelligently about your life every moment of every day.

That is not to say, there will not be days when you may want to give up on something or someone for that matter. It happens. But, before you do that, it is worth asking yourself, why? Because if the reason for giving up on something or someone subscribes to an old way of thinking, to your old thought patterns, your old behaviors, your old defense mechanisms, your traumas and your projections, chances are, the decision to give up on this or that, or this person or that person, will not be a good decision in the long run. At the moment, I must be honest and say, you can't fully trust your decision-making faculties yet, until you have established a consistency in making good decisions. Only then can you really differentiate between what is a good decision, a truly good decision and what is not. Your mind will try to convince you otherwise until you train it to do something that it is not used to doing at first. It's like establishing credit. You will not get approved to buy a home or a car until you have credit history and a history of good credit, a history of paying your bills on time and so on. Otherwise, lenders will not lend to you because they cannot take the risk on someone without good credit history. Your decision-making can be viewed in a similar way. I would suggest focusing on yourself in terms of doing things which promote self-care, such as taking the time out to think clearly about something. You can sit and meditate on what it is you want to change or do. You can also go for a long walk and consult yourself during that walk. Your gut, your heart and intuition are all there to help you make a good decision. However, it is best to consult those inner faculties first to gather a "gut feeling" or "knowing" or "sense" about something you want to change or do differently in your life. In other words, because your mind is "under construction" in terms of learning to make better decisions, you can count on your gut, your heart and your intuition to help "feel" your way through things, entirely, until the mental faculties responsible for decision-making are dialed in.

This is where grit comes in as well. Because it does take "guts", your "heart" to feel, and a "sense" to know, what it will take to keep you going, to keep you on your path and keep you focused on the objective, whatever that objective is for you. For right now, I believe the objective is learning to make better decisions, to help you break these old patterns and cycles which have kept you locked into a loop like cycle of drama and suffering, stress and anxiety, and fear, in your life. Those are the things that we all inherently do not want to keep manifesting as a life script. In fact, I believe we all are passionate about something and possess the guts to persevere and to prosper as a result of our personal conviction and commitment to ourselves. Like raising children. As a parent, grit is applied often. The gumption to raise your children in a wholesome and healthy family environment, educating them about being honest, caring and thoughtful people, to do the right things, to work hard, to focus on education, and to be a good person in the world, is very gritty.

Raising children to be good human beings in the world is not an easy thing to do. Raising children to do the right things, to be successful at whatever they put their minds to is not easy to do. And to raise your children and support their decisions regardless of whether or not you agree with their choices is very hard to do, I am certain of it. Therefore, when you consider these acts that you perform, these decisions you make for the benefit of your children, you can apply that same effort for you, so that you can benefit from your own efforts as well. It is a win, win for everyone to be honest. When you apply the same effort and energy to your own mental well-being, your mental health and wealth, to your physical health and wealth, to your spiritual health and wealth, to your financial health and wealth, you will be successful in every area of your life. That is not to say, uncomfortable things don't happen, or that bad things don't happen. We know that they do. However, how we choose to approach these events and scenarios, how we choose to counteract them, and how we choose to solve them is entirely up to us. That is what we have control over. We have control over our thoughts, moods, feelings, emotions, decisions and actions.

Moreover, when we consider the concept of GRIT as Angela Duckworth shares in her book, we can, more than likely determine that grit is a theory, a perception, an applicable concept, a philosophy, psychological model for understanding our own behaviors and thought processes, and it is a mantra that we may live by if we so chose. What's more, grit combined with our own character, our heart, our energy, our will, all make for a formidable force for good and doing good in the world. For example, Duckworth states that "one way to think about grit is to understand how it relates to other aspects of character. In assessing grit along with other virtues, I find three reliable clusters. I refer to them as the intrapersonal, interpersonal, and intellectual dimensions of character. You could also call them strengths of will, heart and mind."[91] It is obvious to me that grit is not grit without strength of will, heart and mind. Thus, grit plus, strength of will plus heart plus mind equals formidable force for good. These are all virtues that we all innately possess. These virtues are not for a particular kind of person. They exist inherently in each of us. Every single person is more than capable of accessing these traits, these gifts, these virtues, these tools, if you will. In sum, no one is devoid of these things.

So, when I look upon my life and see all of the times I quit something, or up and left and moved somewhere, or broke up with this person or that person, or ended my marriage, or abandoned a project or didn't follow through on my ideas, or started something and didn't finish it, these are all products of poor decision making, of laziness, of projections, of cyclical thought patterns of, poor patterns of behavior, of control dramas, of poor self-control, of compulsiveness, of subconscious psychobabble, and so on. The question then becomes, do I want to continue living my life like that? The answer, is no. This is not a way to live or to continue living. Because this way of living is damaging. It hurts other people. Its selfish. And it's not healthy for anyone one, myself most importantly. Therefore, it would be in my best interest to consider the GRIT theory as an application, a philosophy, an art form for self enhancement and personal growth, a mantra for spiritual advancement and evolution, a continual work in motion for my entire life. And I do believe that you can do the same. You can adopt the GRIT theory and change the trajectory of your life, simply by making the decision to embrace your innermost "grittiness"! This is the first "active" step forward on your yogic path to self-realization and personal freedom!

---

[91] Duckworth, Angela, *GRIT: The Power of Passion and Perseverance*, (p. 273)

Chapter 16

Subconscious Mind Theory

In the beginning stages of my yoga journey, I was prompted to read the book *The Power of Your Subconscious Mind* by Dr. Joseph Murphy, in 2005. It was one of several books I was prompted to read. But this one book changed many things for me. This one book shifted how I perceived the world around me and my relationship to it. Most importantly, it shifted how I perceived my own mind, my behaviors, thoughts, my decisions, my intentions, my interactions with others, how I communicated with others and how I communicate with myself in terms of positive "self-talk". In other words, this particular book allowed me to examine the important role in which the subconscious mind plays regarding how I experience life on daily basis, and how I, through conscious choices and good decisions, can change my life experiences, my relationships with other, my interactions and focus on the things I would like to see changed and materialize. The-power-of-the-subconscious-mind-theory, certainly afforded me the opportunity to investigate this concept on an intimate level pertaining to my personal thoughts, feelings, emotions and decisions. In sum, the perspective offered in the book was the perspective of considering the subconscious mind in a new way, which placed me directly in the driver's seat of my own conscious thoughts and experiences.

For example, Dr. Murphy asserts that "William James, the father of American Psychology, said that the power to move the world is in your subconscious mind. Your subconscious mind is one with infinite intelligence and boundless wisdom. It is fed by hidden springs and is called the law of life. Whatever you impress upon your subconscious mind, the latter will move heaven and earth to bring it to pass. You must, therefore, impress it with right ideas and constructive thoughts."[92] What's more, "the reason there is so much chaos and misery in the world is that so many people do not understand the interaction of their conscious and subconscious minds. When these two principles are in accord, in concord, in peace, and synchronously together, you will have health, happiness, peace, and joy. There is no sickness or discord when the conscious and subconscious work together harmoniously and peacefully."[93] Notably, "whatever thoughts, beliefs, opinions, theories, or dogmas you write, engrave, or impress on your subconscious mind, you will experience them as the objective manifestation of circumstances, conditions and event."[94] How, you may ask does this happen? "Your thought is received as a pattern of neural firings in your cerebral cortex, which is the organ of your conscious reasoning mind. Once your conscious or objective mind accepts the thought completely, it is transmitted to the older parts of the brain, where it becomes flesh and is made manifest in your experience."[95] In other words, when Dr. Murphy says, "it becomes flesh" what he means is that your thoughts become "real" or become a "reality".

Proverbs 23:7 asserts that "whatever a man thinketh, so is he." Similarly, there are countless "proverbs", quotes, sayings and teachings that all point to this statement of our thoughts becoming "things". You have heard that phrase before as well, I am sure. Moreover, in the world of Positive Psychology, this particular message is part of their fundamental therapeutic efforts to help those understand the power of their own thinking. One could argue that Dr. Murphy himself subscribed to the

---

[92] Murphy, Joseph, Dr., *The Power of Your Subconscious Mind*, (p. 39)
[93] Murphy, Joseph, Dr., *The Power of Your Subconscious Mind*, (p. 39)
[94] Murphy, Joseph, Dr., *The Power of Your Subconscious Mind*, (p. 38)
[95] Murphy, Joseph, Dr., *The Power of Your Subconscious Mind*, (p. 38- 39)

school of Positive Psychology. Perhaps he was. Because the essence of this message could not be more apparent, when we consider the outcomes of our lives influenced by our decision-making be those decisions good or not so good. What's more, what Murphy suggests in his book is you and I are fully capable people able to change how we can experience life in a positive, harmonious, healthy and fulfilling way. These concepts are subscriptions of Humanistic Psychology for which we had discussed. However, it is one thing to acknowledge the concepts for which Murphy suggests and it is another to actually commit oneself to doing the work so that one could realize the benefits associated with using one's subconscious mind actively, consistently, persistently and continuously. And it can be a grueling process when our society is filled with negative stories, collective negative thought patterns, naysayers and pessimists. You have to work through the block of negative thinking, negative actions, negative words and negative feelings from those around you, from people you may know, from the news, from everything so that you are not derailed.

Murphy suggests that you can counteract negative suggestions. For example, Murphy states that when you "pick up the paper or turn on the television news. Every day, you hear dozens of stories that could sow the seeds of futility, fear, worry, anxiety, and impending doom. If you accept them and take them in, these thoughts of fear can cause you to lose the will for life. However, once you understand that you do not have to *accept* them, choices open up for you. You have within you the power to counteract all these destructive ideas by giving your subconscious mind constructive auto-suggestions."[96] Additionally, "check regularly on the negative suggestions that people make to you. You do not have to be at the mercy of destructive heterosuggestion. All of us have suffered from it in our childhood, in our

---

[96] Murphy, Joseph, Dr., *The Power of Your Subconscious Mind*, (p. 27)

teens, and in adulthood. If you look back, and you can easily recall how parents, friends, relatives, teachers, and associates contribute in a campaign of negative suggestions. Study the things said to you, closely examine their underlying meaning, and you will discover that many of them were nothing more than a form of propaganda. Its concealed purpose was—and is—to control you by instilling fear in you."[97] Lastly, he purports that "this heterosuggestion process goes on in every home, office, factory, and club. You will have that many of the suggestions people make, whether they know it or not, are aimed at making you think, feel, and act as they want you to, in ways that are to their advantage, even if they are destructive to you."[98]

I will stop there and help clarify Murphy's meaning regarding "propaganda" and that people are "making you think, feel, and act as they want you to, in ways that are to their advantage." Though I do not entirely agree with that last statement, as if people are meaning to cause harm to another intentionally, we can both probably agree that some people, not all people, are going through what you and I are going through and whatever is said is not intentional. We can also, more than likely agree, that some people are unconsciously and subconsciously behaving, thinking, acting, speaking and making decisions rooted in traumas, pain, suffering, anger, resentments, unresolved issues, or perhaps there is a mental health issue present that has not been fully diagnosed. There are all sorts of reasons why some people behave poorly, say negative things, do things which may cause harm to another or to themselves. And perhaps some small number of people actively seek to harm others intentionally. However, many people, I believe, genuinely wish to feel loved, to be loved and to be happy in their

---

₉₇ Murphy, Joseph, Dr., *The Power of Your Subconscious Mind*, (p. 28)
₉₈ Murphy, Joseph, Dr., *The Power of Your Subconscious Mind*, (p. 28)

lives. But for a number of people, misery has become a very close friend and misery is the shadow which follows some people around and inserts itself into conversations, into one's behavior, thinking and so forth. All of this to be said, this is where the hardest kind of work must be done, which is to counteract all of the many negative thought forms swirling around in the atmosphere of your life, through people you may know or not know, at the workplace, at home, on the news, in the paper, in social media, especially social media. You may have to work a little harder to combat those negative suggestions by immediately replacing those suggestions with positive suggestions each and every second of the day until that action becomes second nature to do so and your mind automatically operates in a counteractive way on its own without you having to work so hard for it.

The, subconscious-mind-theory, can be used in actuality. The theory only remains a theory until theory is supported by scientific evidence. And the scientific evidence, will be the result of your willingness to try using your own subconscious mind through the activity of thought replacement practices such as actively replacing a negative thought with a positive thought. Moreover, the scientific evidence can be the result of your willingness to try using your own subconscious mind through the activity of "positive self-talk" practices. For example, when you begin talking to yourself, which we all do, and that talk is negative, meaning, you belittle yourself, saying things like, "I'm not enough", "I'm not that smart", "I can't do it", "I'm a failure", "I'm not talented enough", or "that person is better than I am" at this or that, then you are actively engaging in "negative self-talk" practices, which then becomes part of your conscious thinking landscape which then gets deposited into your subconscious mind, which then becomes a replay of those very things, experienced in real time—in reality, like a loop or a broken record. These are the chain of events that occur as a result of unconscious negative self-talk practices, practices you may not have even been made aware of until just this moment. And while you are probably reflecting on times that you have done this you may begin to see the chain of events which unfolded in your reality at that time. There is a pathology to thought patterns. Hence, when the thought patterns persist your decision-making is influenced, with a probability of decisions being poor, in quality, most consistently.

Notably, the outcomes in our lives are a result of our decisions more often than not. The outcomes in our lives are a result of our thought processes, thought patterns, patterns of negative thinking, patterns of negative behaviors and of negative reactions to events which happen in the moment because our projections are right there with us, our misery is right there with us infused in our "reactions" to this and that, and in our communication with others, so on and so forth. And when we are "triggered" in an interaction with someone, or by something, we have to stop right there and begin asking ourselves, why do I feel this way? Or why am I reacting this way? Or where is this coming from? Because there is a genesis. There is a beginning point. We can trace the trigger to the origin or source. Much like how an epidemiologist starts with ground zero of when a virus has struck a region of the world and traces it back to an original source or origin point at which the virus first manifested. And for the sake of this particular discussion, let us review what epidemiology is to some degree. Firstly, "Epidemiology is the study and analysis of the distribution, patterns and determinants of health and disease conditions in defined populations."[99]

In this case, regarding our "triggers" we have to study and analyze the distribution of thoughts leading up to the "trigger", our thought patterns, and determinants of negative thoughts and negative behaviors of

---

[99] *Wikipedia*: https: wikipedia.org/wiki/Epidemiology

our own consciousness. This process of tracing back to the origin point may take minutes to days to weeks. In some cases, months and even years. But with time and practice, the act of "thought-tracing" will become second nature to do so until your mind operates this way on its own without much work or effort on your part. In the beginning, however, this process will require patience. You will need to be patient with the process, be persistent with the process, be determined to follow through. Moreover, it will take "grittiness", guts, gumption, heart, will, and mind. The action of thought-tracing, as it pertains to the subconscious mind, can be a useful when it comes to "reprogramming" your subconscious mind, once you have found the source of your true irritation, your true discomfort, your true disappointment, your true anger and or true sadness. Once you have found the source of whatever it was that "triggered" you to "react" a way, making a "snap" decision, out of "habit", you can replace those negatives with some positives. But you have to be repetitive in your efforts.

For instance, when you have found the origin of your suffering, you can write down a mantra, something that you can repeat verbally over and over again until it gets deposited into your subconscious mind. You can do this before going to sleep because that is when our subconscious mind is most active. If we fill our conscious mind with a positive mantra counteracting the negative thought forms from childhood for example, before we go to sleep each night for as long as necessary, our subconscious mind will latch onto this new information, playing it back to itself over and over again, until your mantra becomes a new reality for your, until it is played back to you in real-time. At which point, you will have more control over your decision-making process, and behavior overall. We can certainly apply this logic to any other kind of "trigger" or event, circumstance, or situation as they unfold in the moment. By applying the subconscious mind theory, the path to self-realization and personal freedom strengthens.

Chapter 17

Spiritual Being Theory

I must admit how excited I am to share this particular theory as it pertains to the decision-making process and behavior. Because this theory, I believe is the one theory which places all of our experiences into proper perspective. This one theory changes our perception of self and the world at large. Simply because, the reality is, as Bob Frissell has titled his book, appropriately, "We are Spiritual Beings Having a Human Experience". This is the book that opened my eyes to a higher way of thinking and perceiving. It was almost as if this book was helping me to graduate to a higher level of self-mastery in a number of impactful ways, ways that I had not anticipated experiencing had it not been for this singular truth. That we are in fact, spiritual beings having a human experience. However, for some, this concept is very far reaching and seemingly nonsensical. And in some ways, the idea that we potentially are spiritual beings having a human experience, does seem far out. Conversely, I do believe that we are. Why? Because this body and brain of ours is temporary, it is finite. It cannot come with us, wherever we go next, if you believe in such things. Its nature, or composition, or design, is limited to this domain only, to this reality, to this time and space, to this solar system, this planet, and this world. On the other hand, our essence, spirit, energy, light, dark, whatever you want to call the thing that really makes you "you", beyond a personality and beyond persona is infinite and inextinguishable.

Yet, for you to better understand that you are not just your body, and brain, you have to know in your heart, in your bones, in your soul, in your mind, that you *are* a spiritual being once the body perishes and it ceases to exist. If you know that, you are propelling yourself to new heights of consciousness and self-understanding, to newer levels of self-awareness and ultimately, self-realization which is the ultimate gift because freedom resides there. Moreover, to "know" something you have learn something, you have to be educated about that which you have come to know. For example, Bob Frissell asserts that "for the last 13,000 years, as I say, we have been giving our power away; and one of the ways we have been doing that is by thinking that authority lies outside of us. Authority in what sense? Authority in every sense: authority for judging what we ought to do and ought not to do, authority for deciding what is real and what is not real."[100] What's more, "in our present day world, the way we most typically give away our authority is by believing that every area of life is only understood by "experts," people who specialize in some form of knowledge and therefore really know more than we could possibly know about it. We have experts in health and experts in finance and experts in plumbing and experts in how to groom the dog. The average "well-adjusted" human won't make a move without consulting someone whom he things knows more than he does. This expert-trusting-mentality is enormously reinforced by the success of left-brain technology: the ability to predict and control the occurrence of material phenomena by what amounts to little or more than we sophisticated cunning and stealth!" [101]

Taking a moment to drink that in, it is worth noting that some of what Frissell is trying to convey may sound completely radical or potentially unrealistic. And some of what he suggests, I do not entirely agree regarding his general attitude about "experts." To be fair, it is nice to have people out there in the world who have dedicated their time and energy to their craft,

---

[100] Frissell, Bob, *You Are a Spiritual Being Having a Human Experience*, (p. 34)
[101] Frissell, Bob, *You Are a Spiritual Being Having a Human Experience*, (p. 34)

their art, the field of study and so forth. All expert means is that the person dedicated over 10,000 hours of their time to what they do. That is what makes them an expert. And anyone can be an expert at just about anything. For example, if you put 10,000 hours of time into changing your thought processes and decision-making processes, to altering your behavior in order to enjoy positive outcomes, you too, will be considered an expert in behavior modification and thought processes. Just like I am or have become an "expert"[2] because I have dedicated over 20,000 hours of time and practice to changing my thought processes, decision-making process, and to modifying my behavior that inspire positive outcomes in my life more often than not, through yoga. Being an expert is not a bad thing. However, what he is implying with those statements, to better clarify, is that we as people have come to rely too heavily on other people's authority to the point that we have lost touch with our own authority, our own power, our own sense of empowerment. That is what Frissell is trying to convey. Or least, that is what I extrapolate from his message.

Furthermore, the point about authority being given away is something that resonates for me. Because for so long, I felt powerless. I felt like I did not possess the authority within my own mind to stand firmly on my own two feet against the myriad of negative thoughts and negative self-talk and "triggers". Moreover, I felt that I lacked the authority to hold my ground when faced with negative thoughts and talk from others, including their "triggers" and their negative realities in which their subconscious has played back like a loop. I felt helpless for a time, unable to really get a handle on my thoughts, moods, emotions, feelings, decisions and behaviors because I did not reclaim my authority. And this is the chapter which I am reading from. Because personal authority is paramount in the process of good decision-making. You have to feel that you "know" beyond doubt that you are making a solid, informative, critically thought out, good decision about this or that. You cannot waver in your decision-making process. You have to feel confident in your ability to know what is right for you and what is not right for you, but this authority comes into being when you make a proclamation to get it back. You have to take a stand against your own negative thoughts, feelings, emotions, actions, behaviors and decision-making. Because this process is not about anyone else or anything else. It is about you. It is about your own mind and your own life. It is not up to anyone else to solve for you. It is not up to an "expert" to help fix for you. You have to be willing to fix it for yourself and for yourself alone. Not for anyone else, including your children or your spouse. They will benefit from the work you do, but you have to decide to do the work for yourself first and foremost.

Personal freedom comes in the form of personal power, personal confidence, personal authority, and personal empowerment. Personal freedom comes in the form of self-understanding, self-knowing, self-discipline, self-awareness, self-mastery, and self-realization. That is where the true power rests. True power and personal freedom rests in the core of your being, in your heart, in your gut, and in your mind once you have chosen to open that door. Because consciousness is not limited to this reality. Consciousness has the ability to expand. This is what the yogis talk about in their teachings. This is what Patanjali talks about in *The Yoga Sutras*. This is what Sri Swami Satchidananda talks about using various analogies to better explain the Sutras of Patanjali. The conversation about spirituality should not be omitted in this context because it is a vital source of who we are as spiritual beings having a human experience. There is no other way really to look at it in the sense that, we contain all of the spiritual tools, the psychic tools, the psychological tools and the physical tools to change our thinking, to change how we make decisions, to change how we make choices in life, to change how we relate to our own thoughts, to change how we interact with the world, with others, with our loved ones and to change how we wish to experience living our lives each and every day. I think that all of these possibilities are worth pursuing in the form of understanding that we are not without power and authority and that we have to abandon the idea and the ingrained notion that we are without power and authority.

For example, Frissell purports that "another way that we fail to recognize our own authority, our own authorship of our world, is by surrendering the right to evaluate and judge our own activities to our governmental authorities, religious teachers, and to attitudes that are created for us by the media. We believe that how we should behave and what we ought to think, and feel can be determined by rules and interests and images that lie outside of ourselves. We let radio preachers or TV news commentators form our minds. We let advertising images manipulate our attitudes and direct our desires."[102] On this point, I do agree with Frissell that we do allow things outside of ourselves to dictate what is and what is not. We do allow, perhaps unknowingly, or unconsciously, these outside sources manipulate our thought processes and therefore our decision-making process and behavior. Until you become aware, you may not know that these phenomena are happening. Until you become aware you may not even realize that these activities are happening every moment of your life.

The proposition for seeking a yogic path to self-realization and personal freedom is the proposition of considering unconventional possibilities and potentialities. The proposition for seeking an alternative route to better understanding the nature of your mind, how it works and how you can control it, is the proposition of considering various perspectives that may seem unrealistic, or improbable or impractical.

---

[102] Frissell, Bob, *You Are a Spiritual Being Having a Human Experience*, (p. 36)

Because in pursuit of self-realization and personal freedom you must be radical in your thinking, you must do things that other people will not even consider or might criticize. You must think in ways contrary to your ordinary thinking and contrary to the ordinary thinking of your closest friends and family, coworkers and others who engage with you on a day-to-day basis. And it is possible, there will be conflicts of opinion, conflicts of interest and conflicts of perspectives, ideas, and theories. There is a strong possibility that conflicts of this and that may occur as a result of your efforts to improve the quality of your mind, and your life. Naturally, I say, carry on.

Staying the course of any path is not easy to do. Sticking to your proverbial guns to enhance the quality of your life for the better, and to benefit from your good decision-making, will be challenging. I know this first-hand. Sometimes you may experience two steps forward and three steps back. There is that possibility. I cannot promise you that the path you are presently on will be filled with rainbows, sunshine, flowers and fragrance. It will be filled with dark clouds, thorny bushes, thunderstorms, and a fowl odor. You will have to accept the goodness and the uncomfortableness of the path you are on. Because if anyone tells you that your path will be super amazing and you will feel blissful and full of joy from beginning to end, they are lying to you and they have been living in a world of delusions. This path is treacherous. But it will eventually become beautiful. Even the treacherous parts of your path will be thought of as beautiful. Because there, even the ugly is beautiful. Even the grewsome has its own brand of beauty. The path will consist of your most beautiful truths and your beautifully ugly truths.

Yet, in all of these revelations, it is important to remember that you are not reduced only to your physical, emotional, and mental experiences.

Because that is not all there is. The power that you will soon step into is the power in knowing the truth of who you are as a spiritual being having a human experience. That you are not only your struggles, your past, your trauma, your pain, your suffering, your poor decisions. You are more than all of that. But there must be a recognizing of the fact that you are not only those things, which hinge on the physical. The power that you will soon step into is the power knowing that you are so much more than the mere physical. Because in that knowing, in that truth, you can embrace all of the parts that make up the you that you are right now today. And in so doing, you can assert the kind of confidence you that this knowledge inspires to continue on your journey of self-realization.

Moreover, the freedom for which you seek, the liberation that you can experience will not come from the outside world. Freedom will not come from your political beliefs, religious beliefs, your scientific beliefs, your beliefs in non-belief, your esoteric beliefs, your cultural beliefs, your familial beliefs, gender/non-gender beliefs, your medical beliefs and or your technological beliefs. Freedom will not come from any of those beliefs, or belief structures. Freedom comes from within your own mind. Because the shackles are around the mind, not around your ankles and or wrists. So, when the concept of spiritual-being-theory is considered, you are considering the possibility that you have the choice and the option to either embrace that you are a spiritual being having a human experience. And in so doing, there is the chance that your thought process will be influenced by the light of this knowledge for which you have chosen to embrace or deny. Therefore, the authority that you have been giving away to the world over, can slowly return to you, with every passing thought, with every passing choice you make, with every passing favorable decision you make that will lead to yet another favorable decision, resulting in more and more favorable outcomes in your life.

Chapter 18

Blink Theory

Now that we have learned more about having more agency over our sense of authority, and building trust in our decision-making faculties, reasserting our sense of personal power in the world. And another facet of the decision-making process that includes the kind of decision we as a human-beings make in times of stress, processing all sorts of data almost instantaneously, thereby making snap decisions, or gut decisions, or "blink" decisions. This decision-making faculty is instinctive and is a main contributing process which allows us to survive, to fight or take flight, for example. For instance, according to Malcom Gladwell, the author of *Blink: The Power of Thinking Without Thinking*, Gladwell asserts that "the part of our brain that leaps to conclusions…is called the adaptive unconscious, and the study of this kind of decision-making is one of the most important new fields in psychology. The adaptive unconscious is not to be confused with the unconscious described by Sigmund Freud, which was a dark and murky place filled with desires and memories and fantasies that were too disturbing for us to think about consciously. This new notion of the adaptive unconscious is thought of, instead, as a kind of giant computer that quickly and quietly processes a lot of the data we need in order to keep functioning as human beings."[103]

What's more, "the only way the human beings could have ever survived as a species for as long as we have is that we've developed another kind of decision-making apparatus that's capable of making very quick

---

[103] Gladwell, Malcom, "The Internal Computer", *Blink: The Power of Thinking Without Thinking*, (p. 11)

judgements based on very little information. As the psychologist Timothy D. Wilson writes in his book *Strangers to Ourselves*: "The mind operates most efficiently by relegating a good deal of high-level, sophisticated thinking to the unconscious, just as modern jetliner is able to fly on automatic pilot. The adaptive unconscious does an excellent job of sizing up the world, warning people of danger, setting goals, initiating action in a sophisticated and efficient manner.""[104] But there is more to consider regarding our adaptive unconscious making "snap-decisions" for the sake of survival. Particularly when it comes to avoiding danger which is instinctive in and of itself. Whereas when it comes to setting goals for example, we have to use our value-based decision-making faculty. We have to also remember that even in our adaptive unconscious decision-making faculty that that too, needs training. Though, instinctively we duck when a ball is being thrown at our head. Or we go out on a date with someone after a first glance at the individual.

In other words, our adaptive unconscious decision-making process makes snap decisions based on both the immediate data presented in the moment and old data that has been stored in the unconscious mind used as a reference, which could make some snap decisions poor or unfavorable. So if we are talking about our conscious decision making faculty such as value-based decision-making process, the habit-based decision-making process and the adaptive unconscious decision-making process, the conversation should, in my humble opinion, include the quality of each decision-making faculty. Because sometimes, not all snap decisions are sound. Sometimes some people make really poor snap decisions out of fear and anxiety, which causes accidents. Human error is called human error for

---

[104] Gladwell, Malcom, "The Internal Computer", *Blink: The Power of Thinking Without Thinking*, (p. 11)

a reason. Conversely, some snap decisions are good snap decisions. And the argument point Gladwell proposes is that quick, snap decisions are not all bad but are also good and that perhaps human beings spend too much time deliberating about this or that. Of course, I am of the fixed opinion that human beings to do not do enough deliberating and critical thinking to create the best outcome in one's life, given where a number of people are in their lives, which do not inspire or reflect "good decision-making" regardless of whichever faculty was used at the time.

However, Gladwell purports that "we really only trust our conscious decision making. But there are moments, particularly in times of stress, when haste does not make waste, when our snap judgements and first impressions can offer a much better means of making sense of the world. The first task of Blink is to convince you of a simple fact: decisions made very quickly can be every bit as good as decisions made consciously and deliberately. Blink is not just a celebration of the power of the glance, however, I'm also interest in those moments when our instincts betray us."[105] Moreover, Gladwell brings us back around to a singular point in his argument that our instincts do in fact betray us. And as we have already learned, that is because there are a lot of unresolved thoughts and conditions encoded in the unconscious mind that interfere with the snap decision-making process, making even that a bit dark and murky. For instance, Gladwell states that "our unconscious is a powerful force, But it's fallible. It's not the case that our internal computer always shines through, instantly decoding the "truth" of a situation. It can be thrown off, distracted and disabled. Our instinctive reactions often have to compete with all kinds

---

[105] Gladwell, Malcom, "The Internal Computer", *Blink: The Power of Thinking Without Thinking*, (p. 14)

of other interests and emotions and sentiments."[106] Therefore, "when our powers of rapid cognition go awry, they go awry for a very specific and consistent set of reasons, and those reasons can be identified and understood. It is possible to learn when to listen to the powerful onboard computer and when to be wary of it."[107]

I liked that he referred to this portion of his book as "The Internal Computer" because it gives us a really useful way of thinking about what Gladwell proposes regarding the adaptive unconscious decision-making process of the brain. Because even computers get viruses. Computers slow down when the hard drive reaches full capacity. Computers become less optimal and less efficient with time if we do not take them in periodically to get "cleaned up", fixed, or updated. In sum, computers need to be managed and taken care of, so that they run efficiently and optimally. Similarly, if the brain is like a computer, or that the adaptive unconscious is like an internal computer, then the adaptive unconscious needs updating, cleaning up, adjusting and fixing so that it runs optimally and efficiently. The consequences of not doing so could prove to be problematic over the course of one's life. For example, Gladwell states that "our snap judgements and first impressions can be educated and controlled…Just as we can teach ourselves to think logically and deliberately, we can also teach ourselves to make better snap judgments…The power of knowing, in that first two seconds, is not a gift given magically to a fortunate few. It is an ability that we can all cultivate for ourselves."[108]

---

[106] Gladwell, Malcom, "The Internal Computer", *Blink: The Power of Thinking Without Thinking*, (p. 15)
[107] Gladwell, Malcom, "The Internal Computer", *Blink: The Power of Thinking Without Thinking*, (p. 15)
[108] Gladwell, Malcom, "The Internal Computer", *Blink: The Power of Thinking Without Thinking*, (p. 16)

Taking a moment to pause here and reflect on the concept of snap judgement or as the chapter is called blink-theory, we can surmise that this process like all other processes pertaining to decision-making requires proper cultivation, like growing a garden or a crop, the soil needs cultivating, tending to, watering, and managing in terms of keeping pests from devouring the garden or the crop. If we want something to work efficiently and optimally, there is "work" to be done. Because nothing will come naturally the way we all think it does. Especially when it comes to decision-making at any level. As we have already established, decision-making is a skill which must be learned, like learning a foreign language or math or science. Decision-making, be it "snap judgement", value-based or habit-based, is an art form, like painting, drawing, or sculpting. Decision-making is a tool like a hammer, wrench, forklift, or pully. In fact, there are people who are trained to use a forklift and other kinds of tools, such as plumbers who are trained to use certain tools for the trade of plumbing. The same goes for carpenters, car technicians, internet technicians, and other technicians who are trained in a particular field to learn to use that which is required for the job, or project. The brain and its decision-making faculties, similarly, require a "trained technician" to operate them accordingly, to provide technical support and assistance in an effort to keep things running smoothly, efficiently and optimally.

When I think of the decision-making processes in this manner, like being a technician, I purposefully place myself in a position of power and I am therefore, empowered to do what is necessary to ensure that my decision-making processes are at their best, resulting in good decision-making activities, thereby producing a series of positive outcomes. You see, this isn't about the illusion of control over the outside world. These concepts, ideas, perspectives, notions, theories, psychologies, philosophies, and discoveries are about the certainty of control over the inside world, over your own mental faculties and functionalities which directly influence your everyday experiences both internally and externally. That is what personal freedom is primarily going to embody. Personal freedom is going to embody a number of truths pertaining to your ability to create the kind of life you wish to create based upon the science, the data, the research, the skills, the knowledge and the understanding of what your brain is capable of doing. And from a neuroscience perspective, we can agree that the brain's ability to process data and information, to store data and information, to send neural impulses through the nervous system, signaling sensations and responses, is the most fascinating organ in the entire body, that science still has yet to fully understand. As human beings we continue to discover new things about the brain and its functions, creating new scientific fields of study and testing methods.

Hence, as the technician, the observer, the Seer, the Knower, the authority of your own mind and mental capabilities, you have the power within you to do what is absolutely required to train your mind, to cultivate it like a gardener, to fine tune it, to enhance it through good eating habits, exercise, mind body practices to reduce stress, proper amount of sleep, rest and relaxation, through herbal supplements to help aid in the process of human optimization efforts, through meditation, or tai chi, yoga, or any other kind of martial arts. These are the protocols for which you can apply to your life to enhance your brain and your body. Especially when it comes to movement. Because as we have learned in our current culture, living a sedentary life or having a sedentary lifestyle, more illnesses and diseases have materialized over the last twenty years. Couple that with poor diets, consumption of processed sugar and salt, poor habits such as smoking cigarettes, consuming too much caffeine, excessive drinking, and taking too many pharmaceuticals, all contribute to poor brain and body performance. Particularly, the brain and it's functions and processes. When the brain is doped up on stimulants, alcohol, nicotine, sugar, salt, too much fat, dehydrated from not drinking enough water, suffering from lack of sleep, is stressed, and anxious, producing the wrong amounts of serotonin, and other neurotransmitters, its performance suffers overall, therefore the decision-making processes suffer, the ability to think clearly and critically, suffers—which ultimately leads to a perpetual cycle of poor decision-making, potentially.

Naturally, you have a choice as to what to do next, knowing what you now know. You can continue the journey down this particular rabbit hole, learning more about the decision-making process or stop now, put the book away and forget about everything you just read. You can do that. That would be your decision. However, I may be able to bet money that you are intrigued at the very least to continue and see where this all goes. Perhaps you are now somewhat convinced of the fact that poor decision-making at least "happens" to everyone. And in some cases, perhaps more than "some", poor decisions happen to some more than others. Perhaps you may identify with the group in which poor decisions happen more often than others. That is ok. I too, am in the same boat. So let us continue to paddle this boat down river, coasting along gaining as much momentum as we can to further ourselves in the knowledge that our decision-making process can certainly be altered and enhanced for the benefit of everyone. Not just you or I, but for those around us, our friends, family, coworkers, fellow students, and so forth. Because as I mentioned before, that when you are better, everyone else around you is better. When you are not at your best everyone else around you, suffers. Therefore, self-care is critical and must be, for your own survival and sanity, be part of your daily ritual. And the self-care methods for which I speak, pertain to things like going for long walks, eating healthy meals, exercising, staying hydrated, getting enough sleep, practicing yoga and or whatever helps you be a better you.

Chapter 19

Better Brain Theory

We have arrived to one of my favorite theories pertaining to the decision-making process—better-brain-theory, which has all to do with things that enhance the brain's function. And when it comes to this particular theory, I enjoy diving down numerous rabbit holes digging along, discovering new concepts to consider and contemplate, new perspectives to ponder and reflect upon, and new methodologies to apply and practice in my everyday life. Brain hacking in a sense has been something of a fascination of mine for the past five years because I have struggled with various brain performance issues such as being overly distracted, attention-deficit hyperactivity disorder, impulse control, obsessive compulsive disorder, anxiety, depression, mood disorder, addiction, codependency, and restlessness. As you can see, I have struggled with a number of mental health issues which have been very difficult to overcome during the past decade or so. Though some of these issues are self-diagnosed based on the symptoms I researched through Mayo Clinic, only one has been "suggested" when I was a child. And the reason I know that I have struggled with the number of issues, is that since my last Ayahuasca ceremony, I have become acutely aware of the fact that my brain, prior to these ceremonies, was not as well as I thought. Since these ceremonies, cognition, decision-making processes, neural functions, and overall performance have dramatically improved. I can sit for hours upon hours reading and writing. My thinking is sharp, my ability to process information is crisp, and most importantly, my decision-making processes are evolving.

However, I do not advocate plant-medicine as a remedy or a cure for anything. And I do not recommend anyone participate in any kind of mind altering ceremony unless one is "called" to do so . Meaning, you have already been thinking of participating in a ceremony long before this book came to your attention. Otherwise, I would say to you, if you are interested in this experience, I suggest doing some research first. I do not recommend making a "snap decision" about plant-medicine without learning all that you can about it first. Not that I discourage you or anyone else from considering plant-medicine rituals. But I do discourage impulsivity when it comes to plant-medicine rituals. Far too many people go to places and participate in these types of ceremonies and do not have very good experiences, and or come back from a remote location in which they visited only to feel haunted by the things they have experienced during their psychedelic excursion. Therefore, for the sake of this chapter, let us focus on other more accessible methods to enhancing your brain performance. That being said, Dr. Sanjay Gupta, a man of many talents has recently published a book called *Keep Sharp: Build a Better Brain at Any Age*. And in this book, he discusses the various ways in which you can build a better brain at any age, as the title suggests.

For example, in chapter 4 "The Miracle of Movement", Dr. Gupta writes "when people ask me what's the single most important thing, they can do to enhance their brain's function and resiliency to disease, I answer with one word: exercise—as in move more and keep a regular physical fitness routine. Maybe you expected me to say diet, crossword puzzles or higher education, but it is all about physical movement. Truth is, even if you've never maintained a consistent workout in the past, you can start today and have quick and significant effects on your brain's health (and your whole body, obviously). Fitness could very well be the most important ingredient to living as long as possible, despite all the other risk factors you bear—age and genetics included. And while it may seem hard to believe, exercise is the only behavioral activity scientifically proven to trigger biological effects that can help the brain."[109] What's more Dr. Gupta asserts that "we cannot yet say exercise will reverse cognitive deficits and dementia, but evidence is mounting to heed the advice that we all would do well to follow: get in motion. Remember: a body in motion tends to stay in motion. And, if you have not been exercising, starting today can significantly protect your brain later."[110] The point that is clear with Gupta's perspective about exercise is that brain performance is evidence of physical exercise. Which means that when brain performance increases, decision-making processes are positively affected, our moods improve, anxiety and depression diminish, and our focus and attention are strengthened.

Though I am a little bias about many of Gupta's points and perspectives because he truly is a brilliant man, anyone can agree that simply moving, walking, riding a bike, movement in general increases brain performance. And though there is a growing body of research to further support this claim, most doctors will agree that daily exercise will help their patient's overall health. Any doctor or medical professional will suggest diet and exercise. These two activities, generally speaking, by and large, are widely accepted and highly promoted activities in the medical community. With that in mind, we cannot argue otherwise honestly. Moreover, when it comes to the enhancement of brain performance as it pertains to the decision-making processes, simply making the decision *to* exercise is yet another first step in the sequence of making good decisions, all producing favorable outcomes. And that is the point of this book, of this chapter, of these theories, is to help you to see how making a change here and an

---

[109] Gupta, Sanjay, M.D., *Keep Sharp: Build a Better Brain at Any Age*, (p. 97)
[110] Gupta, Sanjay, M.D., *Keep Sharp: Build a Better Brain at Any Age*, (p. 97)

adjustment there, will serve you in the long run, and will help change the trajectory of your life course. Because that is the ultimate goal here. That is the reason why you have chosen to read this book in the first place I imagine.

Because again, you and I can agree that when it comes brain performance, we have to consider the biology of the brain and how it does what it does to some extent to better understand our own brain's functionality and why exercise helps the brain to perform better. For instance, Gupta purports that "the biology of how exercise benefits brain health goes far beyond the reasoning that it facilitates oxygenated blood flow, delivering nutrients for neural cell growth and maintenance. We've known for a long time that cerebral blood flow is a good thing. The latest science behind the magic of movement in protecting and preserving brain function, however, is worth understanding and less known among the general public. Again, there are generally two ways that exercise benefits the brain. For one, exercise effectively uses circulating blood sugar and reduces inflammation while stimulating the release of growth factors, substances that promote both the proliferation and function of cells."[111] What's more, "In the brain, these growth factors support the health of new neurons, the recruitment of blood vessels, and the survival of all neurons. The other way that exercise can benefit the brain may seem a little less objective, but it is no less important. We now know that regular movement measurably reduces stress and anxiety while improving sleep and mood—all of which can also positively affect brain structure and functions."[112]

There is certainly a lot to unpack with regards to the biology of the brain, however, the purpose of sharing these bits of information is to help

---

[111] Gupta, Sanjay, M.D., *Keep Sharp: Build A Better Brain at Any Age*, (p. 107)
[112] Gupta, Sanjay, M.D., *Keep Sharp: Build A Better Brain at Any Age*, (p. 107)

provide more clarity as to why exercise is important in terms of brain activity and brain function. In fact, Gupta pulls from his own experience and states that "exercise helps me think better and consolidate new information. Without it, I find that most of what I think are my "new" thoughts are basically a repacking of old ideas. With my brain on exercise, I find that am more likely to have truly novel thoughts, an incredible feeling." In sum, new neural pathways are being created as a result of consistent exercising. And the kinds of exercising can be just about anything. For instance, Gupta purports that "exercise includes a combination of purposeful aerobic cardio work (e.g., swimming, cycling, jogging, group exercise classes), strength training (e.g., free weights, resistance bands, gym machines, mat Pilates, lunges squat), and routines that promote flexibility and balance (e.g., stretching, yoga). It also includes leading a physically active life throughout the day (e.g., taking the stairs instead of the elevator; avoiding prolonged sitting; going for walks during breaks; engaging in hobbies such as dancing, hiking, and gardening)."[113]

So, what is the take-away? The take-away is, movement is life. Movement will change how your body and brain perform. Movement lubricates the joints, regenerates cells and fluids, reduces inflammation, repairs tissue, strengthens muscles and other tissues, increases blood flow, increases oxygen in the blood and brain, which then increases better balance of neurochemicals, neurotransmitters, and neurohormonal secretions, which all effect mood, emotions, thinking processes, and, of course, decision-making processes. The evidence is undeniable and hard to ignore in the face of facts pertaining to our past poor decision-making and perhaps the unfavorable directions our lives took over the course of our life. That

---

[113] Gupta, Sanjay, M.D., *Keep Sharp: Build A Better Brain at Any Age*, (p. 111)

is not to say, however, that somewhere in our lives, good decisions were not made. Of course, we made some good decisions. Everyone does. Some more than others. All I am proposing for myself at least, is being one of those "some more than others" people who make good decisions, rather than being one of those "some more than others" people who make poor decisions in life. Because if there is one thing, I can say about my life regarding the various decisions made and the suffering I caused myself, is that most of the suffering caused was a result of the poor decisions I have made in my life, in my teens, twenties, thirties and forties. I am now forty-eight, and I am just now "getting it", as they say. It only took this long to "figure it out", but I got here.

But the reason I have arrived at this place of self-realization and personal freedom is because I decided long ago that it was time to change my life around and start making good decisions or I was not going to have a good life filled with love and joy, activities, events, prosperity and adventures. I knew that if I remained locked inside my head space the way that it was, I was going to remain stuck in misery for the rest of my life, blaming the world for my problems. And that just isn't a way to live. I refused to believe that is a way to live and that we are all here to be miserable people, struggling, merely surviving and existing. I just could not stomach the thought of going another day the way I was going. It was no longer an acceptable way to continue living my life. And once I reached that very low point in my mind, I asked for help, in the form of a thought. And help came in the form of a phone call from a relative telling me to stop blaming the world for my problems and to do something about it. And as a result of that one telephone call, I was inspired to take a leap of faith and get off my butt and do something radical, unusual and out of character, at least for me given the fact that I had never meditated, never practiced yoga, and never chanted. But I did all of those things to see if they would help me. And they did. I did not expect them to. But they did. In fact, I had my doubts. I just was not entirely sold on the idea of chanting and meditating, but I committed myself to these tasks for a month to see what would happen.

As a result of taking that first step to set up a space in the hallway of my home, with cushions to sit on, candles, prayer beads, and incense, I began my Nichiren Buddhist practice, which later evolved into Yoga. I decided to read books. A lot of books. I decided to say "yes" to the journey and actively and consciously took steps to continue on my mission. One decision led to another decision, which then led to many more decisions, which led to many more favorable outcomes. I decided to start getting up earlier with the dogs and go for long walks in the morning. Following my long walks, I started my Buddhist practice, and then a yoga practice. This was my morning ritual for years. The exercise activities were walking and stretching. Pretty much what I still do now. Only, I have added weightlifting, and strength training. I added these two activities into my life in 2016. Then in 2017, I studied to become a Certified Personal Trainer.

The one thing that can be said about building a better brain essentially, is that there are multiple ways in which to do so. Exercise is one way. Eating better is another. Getting enough sleep is another. Having a mind body practice is also another way. And taking the time to "think" things through, slowing down that process, and not rushing into anything. What's more, doing what I can to recognize when I start falling into a pattern. Because patterns are so ingrained it is hard to notice them once in them. You have to constantly observe your thoughts. But these are just some of the ways in which you can begin to change how you think and perceive the world, and how you can influence your own decision-making for the better. Because there are no rules here. You can design you thinking any way that makes sense for you!

Chapter 20

The Presence Theory

We are nearing the end of our journey together, learning about a number of exciting concepts, theories and applications regarding our behavior and our decision-making process. Of course, once you have completed reading this book, I do not expect that you will start changing everything in a single day. Of course, it is my hope that the moment you began reading this book, you took the first small step to making imperceptible and incremental changes in your attitude, thinking and perhaps decision-making. Because as they say, Rome wasn't built in a day. And "change" is not going to take place in a single read. It will take place over a period of time. But most importantly, "change" will be small, incremental, and imperceptible, as I previously mentioned. It will be a "nudge" here and a "nudge" there to think differently and behave differently. In other words, given a large swath of time, you will notice the gross changes. However, over a shorter period of time, the changes will be very subtle. But to the keen eye, even the subtle changes will be highly noticeable. And the keen eye for which I speak, is your keen eye. Not anyone else's keen eye. Because the only person that mattes here is you. You have to be the one who decides what is best for you. Not me, not this book, not a Tedtalk, not a podcast, not your significant other, or employer, or priest, or pastor, or yoga teacher, or tax accountant, not anyone. You have to be the one to rely upon when it comes to changing how you think, feel, act, speak, and decide things.

With this in mind, allow me to introduce "presence-theory" as it pertains to the decision-making process. This theory comes from the book

I once read called *Presence: Bringing your Boldest Self to your Biggest Challenges*, by Amy Cuddy, about meeting ourselves where we are, accepting the things that we cannot change and doing the work to change the things we can change in a way that does not create stress, anxiety, a feeling of worry, or that may generate self-doubt, fear and feelings of unworthiness. What Cuddy proposes is taking things slowly, deliberately and incrementally when it comes to changing our thoughts and behaviors. I absolutely agree with her perspectives and her approach. Because that is exactly how it all began to unfold for me. Nothing happened too quickly. Granted, things happened consecutively, consistently and continuously, which gave the appearance that things were happening fast. They were not. They were just "happening". Period.

For example, according to the book, presence can be defined in a number of ways. Three of which are the following: "Presence is removing judgement, walls, and masks so as to create a true and deep connection with people or experiences…Presence is loving people around you and enjoying what you do for them…Presence is being myself and keeping confident, whatever happens."[114] These definitions were provided from other people which Cuddy added to her book to illustrate how others may define "presence." Moreover, Cuddy asserts that "the idea of a permanent, transcendent form of presence grew in philosophical and spiritual soils. As the blogger Maria Popova has written, "this concept of presence is rooted in Eastern notions of mindfulness—the ability to go through life with crystalline awareness and to fully inhabit our experience." It was popularized in the West in the mid-twentieth century by British philosopher Alan Watts, who Popova explains, "argues that the root of our human frustration and daily anxiety is our tendency to live for the future, which is

---

[114] Cuddy, Amy, *Presence: Bringing your Boldest Self to your Biggest Challenges*, (p. 23)

an abstraction," and that "our primary mode of relinquishing presence is by leaving the body and retreating into the mind—that ever-calculating, self-evaluating, seething cauldron of thoughts, predictions, anxieties, judgements, and incessant meta-experiences about experience itself."[115]

Notably, the definition of "presence" as Cuddy describes is "*the state of being attuned to and able to comfortably express our true thoughts, feelings, values, and potential.* That's it. It is not a permanent transcendent mode of being. It comes and goes. It is a moment-to-moment phenomenon."[116] And I think you and I can agree that her definition, her meaning and her perspective is something that we can support and actually apply to our own lives. Because what Cuddy is proposing with presence-theory is something that is doable, manageable and sustainable. Moreover, Cuddy's approach to achieving presence is *time conscious*. Meaning, that every small incremental thing that you do for yourself to alter your way of thinking and behaving, will take time. And I used the words *time conscious* instead of "time consuming" because time consuming may sound negative. Time conscious, on the other hand, allows you to be more aware of the process and the time in which the process will take regarding how best to consider your efforts which performed over a period of time, will yield the best results. I know that's a lot to consider. However, when we consider the long-term, taking those small steps now will accumulate over time, like putting $200 a month into your savings account over a period of five, ten and fifteen years. Over time, it will all add up!

Similarly, when we invest a percentage of our time dedicated to making small changes in our attitude, thinking and behavior, over a period of three months, twelve months, two years, five years, and ten years, will all

---

[115] Cuddy, Amy, *Presence: Bringing your Boldest Self to your Biggest Challenges*, (p. 24)
[116] Cuddy, Amy, *Presence: Bringing your Boldest Self to your Biggest Challenges*, (p. 24)

add up! You will certainly profit from your investment almost immediately in this case. You will not have to wait too long to see your interest accrue in this instance. And I equate what you are doing to the world of finances. Because the one thing I know human beings care greatly about is money. Our finances play a very big role in each of our lives. And as long as we are judicious about our finances, smart about our spending, frugal, aware of investment trends and the stock market, and so forth, we make favorable decisions about our finances so that we are in the best possible place financially. Similarly, our behavior and decision-making play a very big role in each of our lives. And as long as we are judicious about our decisions and behavior, smart about our decision-making process, frugal, aware of the behavior patterns and trends, and behaviors and decisions of others, and so forth, we make favorable decisions about our lives so that we are in the best possible place experientially.

All of that to be said, the first thing that we can do or that you can do right now is begin to slow down your decision-making process. For example, Cuddy asserts that "first, slowing down is a power move. Just as speaking slowly, taking pauses, and occupying space are related to power, so, too, is taking your time to figure out how to respond and slowing down your decision-making process in high-pressure moments."[117] In other words, "slowing down is just another kind of expansion."[118] Cuddy shares her personal experience regarding feeling pressured and panicked and how that just does not seem to work out well. Cuddy states, "because here's the thing about my rushed, panicked response pattern: like making myself physically small, it was an expression of feeling powerless, and it always backfired. Why rush to make what will likely be a poor decision when stress

---

[117] Cuddy, Amy, *Presence: Bringing your Boldest Self to your Biggest Challenges*, (p. 250)
[118] Cuddy, Amy, *Presence: Bringing your Boldest Self to your Biggest Challenges*, (p. 250)

is already preventing me from operating on all cylinders? That's not boldness; it's just reactivity." [119] So, we can surmise based on this perspective that, slowing down our decision-making is beneficial especially when we are feeling stressed or anxious. Another consideration is to not decide at all in the moment. In other words, do nothing. Cuddy was advised on this in a story she shared. First, it was to, slow-down the decision-making process and second it was to do nothing. For instance, Cuddy states, that "second, and this may sound kind of weird: do nothing was doing something. It tempered my feeling of threat. Doing nothing reminded me that I do have some power to slow the runaway train. And it freed me to see and respond to the situation with fully functioning cognitive machinery—better working memory, greater clarity, and the ability to adopt several different perspectives. Not only was doing nothing, doing something, doing nothing was also much *better* than doing something, at least the kind of something I'd been doing."[120]

I like this concept of "doing nothing." I subscribe to the Art of Doing Nothing. In Italy, for example, there is a phrase which many Italians live by, as a cultural motto in a manner of speaking. This phrase in Italian is called, *Dolce Far Niente*—The Sweetness of Doing Nothing. I heard this phrase in the movie *Eat, Pray, Love* and thought, "I love it!" Why? Because, in our American culture, we do not live by this kind of motto. Our cultural mottos are things like "No Pain, No Gain" or "Go Hard or Go Home" or "Work Hard, Play Hard." As you can see, pain, gain, going hard, working hard, playing hard, or just accepting the "hard" nature of everything or that gain is not gain without pain, are ideas and cultural concepts we have accepted and adopted in our way of living and thinking, being and deciding.

---

[119] Cuddy, Amy, *Presence: Bringing your Boldest Self to your Biggest Challenges*, (p. 250)
[120] Cuddy, Amy, *Presence: Bringing your Boldest Self to your Biggest Challenges*, (p. 251)

Not that there is anything wrong with these concepts, entirely. They do have value. However, how far to do we go with thinking this way? Because not every situation requires this kind of thinking. On the contrary, some situations do require, the sweetness of doing nothing. But to think this way, in our fast paced, instant gratification world we live in, is almost blasphemous in a way. Moreover, when we consider the act of doing nothing, in some cases, one may perceive that act as an act of laziness and of "not doing the work." However, there is value, in some cases, in doing nothing. Additionally, the concept and activity of "doing the work" is only worthwhile if "doing the work" also reflects a balance between "doing the work" and "doing nothing."

Taking a pause here to digest what we have covered so far, you may begin to think about instances where you could have taken the time out to slow down your decision-making process or taken the time to just "do nothing" or not decide on anything in the moment. And of course, every single human being could reflect on these ideas and agree, that there was a time or two or three or many, that slowing down would have been more beneficial or that by not making a decision on the spot would have been beneficial. But as they say, it's better to arrive to the party late than not at all. And in this case, we can certainly make a cameo appearance and start interacting with all of the party goers such as our thoughts, feelings, emotions, tendencies, patterns and decision-making processes. You do not have to avoid making changes in your life because you think, "it's too late for all of that." It's never too late to change the things that you can. And you can start slowly, incrementally, and nudgingly. Which brings me to my final concept regarding presence-theory.

Cuddy states that "around 2005, a group of economists and psychologists began to explore the notion, based on the results of many studies, that the best way to change people's behavior for the better might not be to request or demand big changes in attitudes and preferences but to subtly, almost imperceptibly, nudge people in a healthful direction. The tactics of this approach are neither dramatic nor bold, and the changes produced are in the beginning, conservative. But over time, the changes spread and fortify. They incrementally build upon themselves, ultimately changing not only behavior but also attitudes and even social norms, which reinforce and extend behavioral changes throughout and across communities. They become the new status quo."[121] What's more, "nudges are effective for several reasons. First nudges are small and require minimal psychological and physical commitment... Second, nudges operate via psychological shortcuts." [122] Lastly, "self-nudges...are minimal modifications to one's own body language and/or mind-set that are intended to produce small psychological and behavioral improvements in the moment. They are tiny tweaks with the potential to, over time, lead to big changes...When you give yourself a self-nudge, the gap between reality and goal is narrow; it's not daunting, which means you're less likely to give up. As a result, your behavior change is more authentic, lasting, and self-reinforcing."

I shall close this chapter, leaving you with those perspectives to contemplate for a moment or two before flipping to the next page. Because I could not agree more with her methodology and thinking, pertaining to the decision-making process and behavior. Self-nudges, small acts, slowing down and in some special cases, doing nothing, are all manageable efforts that in time completely liberate you and place you in a most advantageous position of experiencing a plethora of favorable outcomes in your life.

---

[121] Cuddy, Amy, *Presence: Bringing your Boldest Self to your Biggest Challenges*, (p. 252-253)

[122] Cuddy, Amy, *Presence: Bringing your Boldest Self to your Biggest Challenges*, (p. 254)

Chapter 21

Not Giving a F*ck Theory

Well, my friend, we have finally come to the final chapter of this book. And I hope that so far, you have learned something new, have been inspired in some kind of way to consider something new, or at the very least, extrapolated that as human beings, there is room for improvement and that learning never stops. With that in mind, let us continue with this new concept, not-giving-a-f*ck-theory, based upon the book *The Subtle Art of Not Giving a F*ck: A Counterintuitive Approach to Living a Good Life,* by Mark Manson. This book is as real as it gets. And though, perhaps, Manson's approach is a bit more "in your face", Manson offers many good points to consider pertaining to our decision-making process, our thought process, our beliefs and our behavior. Because the truth is, not everything is a bed of roses. Life is messy. In Manson's view, "sometimes, things are fucked up and we have to live with it." This is true. Sometimes, things are just not that awesome and we do have to deal with whatever those situations are as they are presented. And yet, even in those moments we are faced with choices, options and decisions. There is no walking away from something as it is happening unless it is something that you absolutely must walk away from because that is the only way the matter can be resolved either temporarily or permanently.

Mark Manson argues in his book that "improving our lives hinges not on our ability to turn lemons into lemonade, but on learning to better stomach lemons. Human beings are flawed and limited—as he writes, "Not everybody can be extraordinary—there are winners and losers in society, and some of it is not fair or not your fault." Manson advises us to get to know our limitations and accept them. This, he says, is the real source of empowerment. Once we embrace our fears, faults, and uncertainties—once we stop running from and avoiding, and start confronting painful truths—we can begin to find the courage and confidence we desperately seek."[123] It is clear that Manson is not necessarily a subscriber of Positive Psychology in the traditional sense. He is a realist. However, Manson believes that if people "do the work" to face the pain and the ugliness, the hurt and the uncomfortableness of one's psyche, that is where the healing can truly take place. And I agree with Manson's perspective. We absolutely must face these things head on. We cannot hide from them or try to hide from them forever. We certainly cannot continue making poor decisions and exhibiting poor behavior because we choose to not address the core issues we have been unconsciously holding onto for decades. Additionally, it is good medicine to accept some things about yourself or I accept some things about myself and to understand that even in my limitations, for example, I have the power of choice, of decision-making and of altering my own behavior. How I approach everything and anything in life, is totally within my realm of immediate control.

For example, when it comes to our decision-making process, our attitudes, our behaviors and our perceptions, there is a little thing called "belief". And our beliefs could either (a), do more harm than good, or (b) create more, good than harm. In other words, what we choose to believe with either improve the quality of our lives or maintain the cycle of poor decision-making, thus producing perpetual unfavorable outcomes. For instance, in the section, "Architects of Our Own Beliefs, Manson invites you to imagine a situational scenario. For example, "take a random person

---

[123] Manson, Mark, *The Subtle Art of Not Giving a F*ck: A Counterintuitive Approach to Living a Good Life*, (inside flap)

and put them in a room with some buttons to push. Then tell them if they do something specific—some undefined something that they have to figure out—a light will flash on indicating that they've won a point. Then tell them to see how many points they can earn within a thirty-minute period. When psychologists have done this, what happens is what you might expect. People sit down and start mashing buttons at random until eventually the light comes on to tell them they got a point. Logically, they then try repeating whatever they were doing to get more points. Except now the light's not coming on. So they start experimenting with some more complicated sequences—press this button three times, then this button once, then wait five seconds, and—ding! Another point. But eventually that stops working. Perhaps it doesn't have to do with buttons at all, they think. Perhaps it has to do with how I'm sitting. Or what I'm touching."[124] This example scenario goes on and on until Manson describes what happens in the end. That people who scored the most points believe "that they discovered the "perfect" sequence of buttons that earned them their points. But the methods they come up with are as unique as the individuals themselves."[125]

In other words, people were doing different things believing that what they were doing to earn the points was the reason why they earned the points. They believed that jumping up and down would earn them points, or that by taping the ceiling a certain number of times would get points. I found this part of the science experiment to be funny. But the point that Manson is trying to make with these situational scenarios of how our mind functions is that belief also dictates behavior. For example,

---

[124] Manson, Mark, *The Subtle Art of Not Giving a F*ck: A Counterintuitive Approach to Living a Good Life*, (p. 120)
[125] Manson, Mark, *The Subtle Art of Not Giving a F*ck: A Counterintuitive Approach to Living a Good Life*, (p. 120)

Manson asserts that "our brains are meaning machines. What we understand as "meaning" is generated by the associations our brain makes between two or more experiences. We press a button, then we see a light go on; we assume the button caused the light to go on. This, at its core, is the basis of meaning. Button, light; light, button. We see a chair. We note that it's gray. Our brain then draws the association between the color (gray) and the object (chair) and forms meaning: "They chair is gray." Our minds are constantly whirring, generating more and more associations to help us understand and control the environment around us."[126] Manson continues offering scenarios regarding how the mind draw associations with various objects and our thoughts, which could be false, inaccurate, based on past events, other people's inaccuracies, false beliefs and so on. In sum, Manson states that "most of our beliefs are wrong. Or to be more exact, all beliefs are wrong—some are just less wrong than others. The human mind is a jumble of inaccuracy. And while this may make you uncomfortable, it's an incredibly important concept to accept, as we'll see."[127]

Though I do agree with most of what Manson is saying regarding how all beliefs are wrong. I do not entirely agree with the perspective that "all beliefs are wrong" in that some beliefs such as the belief that if you or I walk 2.5 miles per day each day, our bodies will be more conditioned, and we will be in a better mood and will have more energy. Or, that if you or I, practice yoga one hour per day, we will have more flexible bodies and an improved outlook on life. These activities, though scientifically proven to have positive effects on the mind and body, are also "beliefs" because you are trusting that by doing these activities every day, something good will

---

[126] Manson, Mark, *The Subtle Art of Not Giving a F*ck: A Counterintuitive Approach to Living a Good Life*, (p. 122-123)
[127] Manson, Mark, *The Subtle Art of Not Giving a F*ck: A Counterintuitive Approach to Living a Good Life*, (p. 122-123)

happen. You believe that by making the choice to engage in healthy activities your brain function will improve, and your heart health will also improve. You believe that if you start making good decisions, that you will experience more favorable outcomes. In other words, you can use the power of belief for good, using the mechanics of the subconscious mind and using sheer will to see things through, thereby improving the quality of your life in every area of your life. So, that said, I do agree that in the more philosophical sense, or metaphysical sense, "belief" has value and has its uses. Though Manson tosses out the entire idea of "belief", which for the sake of his book and for the sake of his message is totally understandable and makes perfect sense, I also feel that it would be worthwhile to provide another layer to the concept of belief so that you have a fuller understanding about the concept of belief in general as it pertains to the decision-making process and behavior.

The truth of the matter is, regarding the concept of belief, most beliefs are not very well suited for the betterment of human beings. The reality is, many belief systems and or systems of belief have caused more harm than good, they have led to wars, they have led to regime changes, they have led to political dissention, racism, sexism, and every other kind of "ism" detrimental to the collective unification of human beings. So, yes, I believe, that many beliefs subscribe to power, control, and fear mongering. Conversely, some healthy beliefs, dare I say, are very useful and can help our fellow human. Such as harboring the belief, that if you or I do good in the world, and make good decisions, good things will happen. That is not to say, bad things do not happen. But the probability of bad things happening could be far less than good things happening, potentially, if we believe what we believe about doing good, having a good attitude and making good decisions. I do not see how any of that can be viewed as a negative to be quite honest.

I think that when we make the effort to change our thinking, to change our behavior, to change our attitude, and to change the way we communicate with others, or to relate to others, to be more compassionate, to be more empathetic, to be more sensitive to a degree to other people's sensitivities, triggers, feelings, perspectives, trauma's and more, we are all better human beings to each other and most importantly to ourselves. I am not suggesting that we have to try and become this whole new person overnight. Not at all. As the title suggests on Manson's book, in many ways, we must embrace the subtle art of not giving a f*ck about what others might think about what opinions other people have, or of other people's hang-ups and negative attitudes, and negative feelings, negative emotions and negative beliefs. We cannot let all of those things into our minds thereby derailing us from our mission of self-improvement. Moreover, we cannot allow ourselves to over-care about other people's issues and problems either. And when I say, "over-care" I mean caring to the point that it causes you suffering, anguish, anxiety, stress, depression, worry and discomfort in your mind and body. That's not natural to be honest. When people do that, I tend to believe that kind of behavior is reflective of guilt on the part of the person caring too much about this or that or about this person or that person. Because I believe that guilt is one of the greatest disturbances of the human psyche.

What's more, guilt pervades most people's every thought when it comes to making decisions or interacting with others. Guilt, shame, and fear, all three of these psychological disturbances create a conscious landscape filled with poor decisions, negative thought patterns, negative emotions and feelings, and ways in which we communicate with others. Guilt, shame and fear pervade relationships, marriages, the family unit as a whole, the workspace, the ways in which countries govern, the ways in which police institutions police communities of color, of communities of lower income, or the ways in which education institutions educate young people in urban areas. Guilt, shame and fear, have caused humanity to plummet into a deep dark abyss of self-sabotage, self-degradation, self-pity, self-destruction, and self-aggrandizement. Therefore, making sound, healthy, well-balanced, good decisions on a regular basis is lost for many. And it was lost on me for decades of my life. Notably, the amount of suffering generated as a result of a series of poor decisions made over decades of time, was astronomical. Again, circling back to my theory of percentages. In my life, about 80% to 90% of my suffering was self-imposed. In sum, I am responsible for most of the suffering I experienced in my life since childhood. Yes, even then. Why? Because the decision-making faculties of my mind were not well developed. I did not learn those skills. I did not cultivate emotional intelligence in my life. I did not learn the art of good decision-making. I was not taught how to do these things. Thereby, acting on impulse most of my life.

Hence, when we consider the effects of long-term poor decision-making, much like how we consider the effects of long-term smoking, we can surmise that these long-term effects are mostly, if not always unfavorable, painful, and hurtful. We know that long-term poor decision-making, much like long-term smoking will cause us to suffer in ways that we may have not considered. But I am here to tell you that you can turn it all around, right here, right now. You are not subject to having to make the same old decisions that cause you pain and suffering. You can do something different. You can think differently, behave differently and so on. You are more than welcome to begin taking the steps you need to take to ensure a better quality of life, simply by making a point to make the kinds of decisions, over a long period of time that will benefit you and benefit those around you. Because when you're better, everyone else around is better!

Closing Thoughts

I am truly grateful for you taking the time to read this book. I hope that it serves you well. I also hope that you have found the value in reflecting upon various aspects of your life or points or moments in your life that you feel things could have perhaps worked out differently if you had made a better decision here and there. Of course, that is not to say that you should dwell on the kinds of decisions you made in the past that rendered unfavorable outcomes. On the contrary, you could use those moments of the past as learning experiences for the present, rendering favorable outcomes for the future. This book is not about dwelling on the past. This book is about objectively reviewing the timeline of your life to see, when it would have been a good time to make a good decision, or at what point making "good" decisions would have helped you. Because the truth is, we cannot make the small changes we need to make when we are stuck in a state of subjectivity of thought. We ought to progress through the practice of objectively thinking about our life and the moments therein. This objectivity of thought will require you to set aside emotion, long enough to "objectively" review, examine, and analyze various experiences as they pertain to the decision-making process. That is all.

You can think of referring to an objective state of thinking like a scientist would think of a science experiment. Of course, the scientist has many things hinging upon the success of an experiment. However, objectivity is the key ingredient in the continuation of experimentation, gathering data, analyzing data, and documenting what one may find. You can consider the timeline of your life as the subject for which you are studying and experimenting with. Not much else needs to go into this experience. You will certainly benefit from reflecting and reviewing your past decisions with a degree of curiosity, optimism, and enthusiasm because you know that by going about this process, suspending judgement, self-doubt, insecurity, guilt, shame and fear, you can accomplish the task of connecting the dots, thereby providing you with the information you need about your own mind, your own thought processes, your own behavior to begin making small tweaks here and there, small adjustments and small changes that all contribute to the greater good, which is You! You are the great good. Realizing this fact, of being the "great good", you are empowered to continue bolstering this belief, and supporting this ideology by way of making consistently good decisions for the betterment and improvement of your life. This process and achievement will be your new superpower. Self-realization and personal freedom will be your new superpowers in life going forward as well. Because that is what this book is about. Helping you to see your potential to be self-realized and to experience the kind of personal freedom which only comes from your willingness to live authentically, completely, and freely in your heart, mind, and body!

Journey well my friend!

Colette Marie

www.ingramcontent.com/pod-product-compliance
Lightning Source LLC
Chambersburg PA
CBHW051449250726
48655CB00001B/326